SAINT JOHN AND
THE SYNOPTIC GOSPELS

SAINT JOHN AND THE SYNOPTIC GOSPELS

by

P. GARDNER-SMITH, B.D.

Fellow of Jesus College, Cambridge

CAMBRIDGE

AT THE UNIVERSITY PRESS

1938

CAMBRIDGE UNIVERSITY PRESS
Cambridge, New York, Melbourne, Madrid, Cape Town,
Singapore, São Paulo, Delhi, Tokyo, Mexico City

Cambridge University Press
The Edinburgh Building, Cambridge CB2 8RU, UK

Published in the United States of America by
Cambridge University Press, New York

www.cambridge.org
Information on this title: www.cambridge.org/9781107601260

First published 1938
First paperback edition 2011

A catalogue record for this publication is available from the British Library

ISBN 978-1-107-60126-0 Paperback

CONTENTS

The author wishes to express his thanks to Mr J. N. Sanders of Peterhouse for his kindness in reading proofs and for his helpful criticisms and suggestions

INTRODUCTION

THIS STUDY may perhaps be considered a waste of labour, for it deals with a subject generally thought to have been settled, a subject on which the voice of scholars ancient and modern has spoken with a somewhat rare unanimity. The critics of to-day have dealt roughly with the opinions of the Fathers in many matters connected with the four Gospels, but they still quote with approval the words of Clement of Alexandria: 'John, divinely moved by the Holy Spirit, wrote a spiritual Gospel on observing that the things obvious to the senses had been set forth in the earlier Gospels.'[1] There are minor differences, no doubt. The traditional view is that St John was acquainted with the work of all the synoptic writers, but the more cautious of modern scholars are inclined to limit his knowledge to the Gospels of St Mark and St Luke, while some, like the late Professor Stanton, think that only dependence upon our Second Gospel can actually be proved. However that may be, there is virtual unanimity in the view that St John, the latest of the evangelists, was to some extent indebted to the work of his predecessors, and although his scheme was essentially original, and he felt in no way bound by the authority of earlier writers, yet he derived from St Mark, or St Mark and St Luke, much of the material which he used in the construction of his own Gospel.

At first sight it seems a reasonable verdict, first a plain story, then meditation thereon. As Dr Inge wrote thirty

[1] Euseb. *H.E.* VI. 14. 7.

years ago: 'We have before us a composition which does not pretend to conform to the modern standard of history or biography, but which does claim to be a true interpretation of the Person and work of Christ, an elucidation of the inner spirit of the new religion, addressed to the Christian Church about a hundred years after the birth of Christ.'[1] St John's Gospel is 'the charter of Christian mysticism'.[2] But even a mystic needs a background of history, and if St John's is indeed the latest of the Gospels (and few have questioned that tradition) it seems safe to suppose that the history embodied in the Synoptic Gospels supplied that background. Indeed, how could it be otherwise? If St Mark wrote in the seventh decade of the first century, and his book was already well known at the time of the composition of the First and Third Gospels, it could hardly have been unfamiliar to the last of the evangelists who, whatever his identity, is not often thought to have written much earlier than the end of the first century.

Many indications are thought to confirm the belief that the Fourth Evangelist had read St Mark's Gospel, and probably St Luke's, though not much definite evidence can be adduced in favour of the belief that he knew the work of St Matthew. In broadest outline he tells the same story as the other three. He begins with the ministry of the Baptist and his testimony to Jesus, just as Mark begins. He tells of the work of Jesus in teaching and working miracles in Galilee and Judaea. He enlarges upon the controversy between Jesus and the Jews, a

---

[1] *Cambridge Biblical Essays*, p. 253.
[2] W. R. Inge, *Christian Mysticism*, p. 44.

controversy which concerned the interpretation of and obedience to the Law. He ends with an extended narrative of the Passion and of the Resurrection. Why should he have adopted this framework, unless he was influenced by the example of Mark?

Moreover, there are thought to be more definite indications of the dependence of St John upon the work of the earlier evangelists. Here and there the Fourth Evangelist refers to persons and places which would only be familiar to his readers if they were already acquainted with such narratives as appear in the other Gospels, and in many places he uses words and phrases which are identical with or very similar to the language of the earlier writers. To most critics this seems conclusive. St John had his own plan, his own aims, and his own methods, but that he was familiar with one or more of the earlier Gospels is generally held to be proved by a close examination of his work. 'By general consent', writes Dr W. F. Howard, 'John used Mark.'[1] Professor Bacon declared that 'John is to Mark in a relation of direct literary dependence', and he went so far as to write, 'John quotes Mark verbally'.[2] Another investigator, Mr E. R. Buckley, says that 'it seems clear that the author of the Fourth Gospel knew St Mark'.[3] The late Professor Stanton concluded that 'the parallels with St Mark certainly seem to afford evidence of an amount and kind sufficient to prove that the Fourth Evangelist knew that Gospel fairly well'.[4]

[1] Howard, *Fourth Gospel*, p. 144.
[2] Bacon, *The Fourth Gospel in Research and Debate*, pp. 366f.
[3] *Introduction to the Synoptic Problem*, p. 271.
[4] *The Gospels as Historical Documents*, Part III, pp. 214ff.

Dr Streeter examined the whole question 'microscopically' in Chapter xiv of his *Four Gospels*, and decided that John is dependent both on Mark and Luke. Similar views might be quoted from many continental critics. It may therefore seem rash, and even presumptuous, to suggest that there is yet something to be said on the other side. The present writer can only say that he has found the usual arguments unconvincing, and that the conviction has grown upon him that there is a case for a fresh examination of the evidence.

Such an examination has been attempted in the following pages. The greater part of the Fourth Gospel has been passed under review, and the question considered whether it is easier to account for the similarities between St John and the Synoptists without a theory of literary dependence, or to explain the discrepancies if such a theory has been accepted.

Many discussions of this question seem to exhibit two faults. In the first place, it is often forgotten that the Church of the first century was largely dependent upon oral tradition for its knowledge of the life of Christ. For many years after the crucifixion no serious attempt seems to have been made to write an account of the ministry of Jesus, and probably the need for such an account was not realized until the first generation of Christians had passed away. But the local churches must have had a great deal of information, and even when allowance is made for the indifference of the early Christians to mere history, we cannot doubt that events such as the baptism by John, the trial before Pilate, the crucifixion and the resurrection, must have been well known before they were described

in any written document. Nor would local traditions
vanish immediately after the publication of the Gospels.
In public assembly the accepted account might be read,
but in oral teaching variants would long survive, and
there would be a natural tendency for every man to tell
a story in the form in which he had learnt it.

This might account for some of the minor variations of
St John from the Synoptists, as it certainly explains some
of the peculiar features of Matthew and Luke. But it may
be doubted whether it is enough to account for the very
wide divergencies which are frequently encountered. On
the other hand, the existence of oral tradition at the time
when the Gospel was written renders the argument for
dependence of St John upon the synoptic writers much
less compelling. Whoever he was, the author of the
Fourth Gospel must have been a member of some local
congregation, and as such he must have been instructed in
the traditions of the Church. It is a fallacy, obvious yet
strangely common, to think that he can only have learnt
about the life of Christ and the incidents of the ministry
from the perusal of some written document.

Secondly, critics who have discussed the relationship of
St John to the synoptic writings have exhibited a curious
tendency to concentrate their attention solely on those
points on which agreement is manifest, and to ignore the
much greater and surely no less significant differences
which require to be explained. Whatever work is con-
sulted, whether it be Dr Streeter's, or Professor Stanton's,
or Professor Bacon's, it will be found that all the emphasis
is laid on such correspondences as may be detected between St John and the other Gospels, and then, when the

question has been decided, some attempt is made to explain the divergencies. Surely the proper method is to take the Gospel as it stands, and, by noting simultaneously both the similarities and the dissimilarities, seek to determine on which side the balance of probability inclines. This may seem a somewhat tedious method, but it is the only way by which an acceptable conclusion can be reached.

Chapter I

JOHN THE BAPTIST

John i

IT IS generally admitted that the Gospel according to St John gives an account of the work and witness of the Baptist which is quite distinctive. Our other sources of information concerning John are Josephus and the Synoptic Gospels, and on the whole these authorities agree fairly well. For Josephus John was a prophet of righteousness;[1] for St Mark he was the voice of one crying in the wilderness, demanding repentance unto the remission of sins, and announcing the coming of One mightier than he. St Matthew agrees, but adds that he proclaimed the nearness of the Kingdom of Heaven. Matthew and Luke both expand the Marcan account of John's preaching, and Luke has some detailed information which does not appear in the First Gospel; but read together Matthew and Luke confirm the representation of Josephus that John was famous as a preacher of righteousness. We may conclude from these accounts read together that John the Baptist summoned the Jews to repent in view of the near approach of some great crisis. How far he connected the coming judgment with the appearance of the Messiah is not so clear, but since judgment requires a judge, there is nothing improbable in the statement of Mark 'And he proclaimed, saying, He that is greater than I cometh after me, the latchet of whose shoes I am not worthy to

---

[1] *Ant.* xviii. v. 2.

stoop down and unloose', or in the addition of Q, 'whose fan is in his hand to purge his threshing floor, and to gather the wheat into his barn, but the chaff he will burn with unquenchable fire'. It is true that Josephus says nothing about an eschatological element in John's preaching, but such an element seems required to explain the note of urgency in his message. It would also help to explain his peculiar practice of baptism, which was not only the natural sign of repentance, but also the seal of admission to the coming Kingdom.[1] However that may be, there can be no doubt that the movement of John the Baptist was of great intrinsic importance. All men held him to be a prophet, and large numbers responded to his call. His position was such that he could effectively rebuke Antipas, and the Tetrarch was impressed by his warning (Mk. vi. 20).

No such picture of John and his work appears in the Fourth Gospel. Probably the Christian Church was little interested in the original traditions of John's ministry except in so far as they seemed to proclaim him the forerunner of Jesus the Messiah. Very soon that aspect of his work would absorb attention to the exclusion of other elements. Even in the Synoptic Gospels we can see where the emphasis is being put, for they base their accounts on the proof-texts quoted from Isaiah and Malachi. But the synoptic accounts are not altogether distorted by Christian interest, and the Q passage incorporated in the First and Third Gospels is sufficiently near to history to give a

[1] Schweitzer, *The Mysticism of St Paul*, pp. 230–237 *et passim*. Schweitzer thinks that 'He that is to come' for the Baptist meant Elijah, the Messiah's forerunner.

picture of the Baptist as a prophet of righteousness in his own right. In the Fourth Gospel, however, tendencies already manifest in Matthew and Luke find more perfect expression. John is no prophet in the Old Testament sense, but a witness whose sole function is to testify to Jesus as the Lamb of God. 'He came to bear witness concerning the Light.' In chapter i there is no mention of John's work as a preacher of righteousness; he declares himself to be the voice of one crying in the wilderness, and his baptism receives only incidental mention: 'Why then baptizest thou, if thou art not the Christ, nor Elijah, nor the prophet?' The author's intention is evidently to lead up to the declaration: 'I indeed baptize in water; in the midst of you standeth one whom ye know not, who cometh after me, the latchet of whose shoe I am not worthy to unloose.'

The points of contact with Mark are (1) the quotation from Is. xl, which the evangelist puts into the mouth of John himself, and (2) the reference to John's successor as one 'the latchet of whose shoe I am not worthy to unloose'. There is nothing here which implies literary connexion. The text from Isaiah was no doubt constantly quoted in the early Church, and the fact that John had prophesied the coming of the Mightier One would be universally remembered. Even so, the phraseology of the Fourth Evangelist is not very close to that of Mark:

Mk. i. 7: ἔρχεται ὁ ἰσχυρότερός μου ὀπίσω, οὗ οὐκ εἰμὶ ἱκανὸς κύψας λῦσαι τὸν ἱμάντα τῶν ὑποδημάτων αὐτοῦ.

Jn. i. 26: μέσος ὑμῶν στήκει ὃν ὑμεῖς οὐκ οἴδατε, ὀπίσω μου ἐρχόμενος, οὗ οὐκ εἰμι ἄξιος ἵνα λύσω αὐτοῦ τὸν ἱμάντα τοῦ ὑποδήματος.

It is to be noticed that St John does not finish the contrast begun with the words, 'I baptize in water', although he refers below to baptism in Holy Spirit (i. 33). Later he states, as the Synoptists do not, that Jesus baptized His disciples—presumably in water (iv. 1).

A certain depreciation of the Baptist and his work has long been recognized as an unmistakable purpose of the Fourth Evangelist, and it is easily accounted for. What is not so often recognized is that there is little evidence that he knew more of the John of history than what he might have learned from the vague traditions of the churches before these traditions became crystallized in the Synoptic Gospels. Let us collect his references. John was sent from God (i. 6); his function was to bear witness (i. 7, 8); he cried 'He that is after me is preferred before me'; he bore testimony to 'priests and Levites' that he was not the Christ, nor Elijah, nor the prophet; he was solely a forerunner (i. 19–24); his baptism was therefore unimportant and hardly worth explaining, it was merely a baptism with water (i. 26). But John knew that his successor was standing among his questioners, and he admitted his own inferiority (i. 27). John also admitted that he did not recognize Jesus by his own insight, and the inference is that the whole purpose of his work of baptizing was to provide occasion for the sign by which the identity of his successor might be revealed. The passage deserves to be quoted at length:

After me cometh a man who is (γέγονεν) before me, because he was before me (πρῶτός μου ἦν). And I knew him not, but in order that he might be shewn forth to Israel, *for this reason I came baptizing in water*. And John bore witness saying, I beheld the Spirit coming down as a dove out of heaven, and resting upon him. And I knew him not, but he who sent me to baptize in water, he said to me, On whomsoever thou seest the Spirit coming down and resting upon him, he it is who baptizeth in holy spirit. And I have seen and borne witness that this is the Son of God (i. 30–34).

Such an account is indeed remote from the synoptic tradition, and it is hard to believe that the author had the written work of Mark or Luke in mind. Behind the Johannine narrative we may discern an outgrown adoptionist Christology, for Christ is the vehicle of the Spirit which remains through baptism the possession of the Church. Most significant for our present enquiry is the explicit denial that John is to be identified with Elijah. The Synoptists were obviously concerned to establish this identification in order to meet Jewish objections to the messianic claims of Jesus. Mark put the plain words into the Lord's mouth, 'I say unto you that Elijah has come' (Mk. ix. 13), and Matthew adds, 'Then the disciples understood that he spake concerning John the Baptist' (Mt. xvii. 13). St John will allow the Baptist no such distinction; he was 'the burning and shining light', but even so his witness was almost superfluous: 'I have a greater witness than John's, the works which my Father hath given me' (Jn. v. 35, 36).

It is easy to see that the Fourth Evangelist, writing for readers who were not greatly interested in the claim that Jesus was the Messiah of Jewish expectation, may have considered the theory that John was Elijah unimportant, or even absurd; but if he had been writing in a Church in which the Gospel according to St Mark was known and esteemed it is most improbable that he would have brushed aside Mark's important contention without a word of argument. The general picture he presents of the work of the Baptist might perhaps be taken as a free development of material derived from Mark, with some elements omitted, and with a new emphasis on certain aspects; but the denial without explanation of an identification prominent in the Synoptists and believed to rest upon the express testimony of the Lord Himself is hard to account'for on the accepted theory. No important dogmatic interest seems to be involved, and it is easier to think that the Fourth Evangelist wrote at a time when traditions about John had not yet been fixed by the acceptance of the written Gospels; indeed, some of the synoptic traditions had not yet been developed.

The latter part of Jn. i relates that two of the Baptist's disciples, hearing his declaration, 'Behold the Lamb of God', followed Jesus and became the nucleus of His disciples. We are not concerned with the historicity of the narrative, which may embody a genuine tradition that the movement of Jesus grew out of that of John and that some of those who had been followers of the Baptist attached themselves to Jesus. But there is surely nothing here to suggest a knowledge of the Synoptic Gospels. Andrew, who hardly appears in the synoptic narratives, is according to John the means of Peter's conversion, and Simon is given the name of Cephas at his first meeting with Jesus.[1] Philip and Nathanael hardly belong to the synoptic tradition at all. Philip is probably the evangelist of Acts viii. 26 ff. rather than the Apostle of Mk. iii. 18,[2]

[1] Cp. Mk. iii. 16, Mt. xvi. 18, Lk. vi. 14.
[2] Bacon, *The Fourth Gospel*, p. 368, note.

and Nathanael is perhaps Dositheus, the leader of the Baptist's followers mentioned in the Clementines.[1] Philip, Andrew, and Peter are said to come from Bethsaida (i. 44), although Mark (i. 29) says that Peter's house was at Capernaum. It may be that 'the discrepancy is unimportant', as Bernard remarks, or it may be that John deliberately substitutes the Hellenized city of Bethsaida for the Galilean town of Capernaum, as Bacon supposes; but the simpler explanation should not be disregarded, that John did not know the Marcan narrative. His apparent contradiction of the earlier Gospel is really pointless.

The whole passage describing the call of the first disciples is irreconcilable with the synoptic accounts. Clearly the evangelist does not intend his narrative to lead up to any such 'call' as that described in Mk. i. 16–20. Jesus says 'Follow me', and henceforth the disciples are found in His company. If St John had heard any such story as that contained in Mk. i, he set it aside, and substituted for it an account more in keeping with his own ideas. But it is more likely that he would have done so if he was acquainted with oral traditions than that he would have contradicted a written Gospel that had already gained currency in the Church.[2]

If the Fourth Evangelist had read St Mark's Gospel its general scheme must have seemed to him entirely unsatisfactory, for he presents an irreconcilable alternative.

---

[1] *Hom.* II. 24, *R.* II. 8: נְתַנְאֵל is the Semitic form of Δωσίθεος.

[2] Streeter thought that certain facts might be explained if Mark and Luke were 'standard works' read in the Church (*Four Gospels*, p. 402). John's account of the Baptist and his disciples represents a strange way of treating standard works!

He leaves no room for any development either in the consciousness of Jesus or in the conception of His Person in the minds of the disciples. The Baptist proclaims Him at once to be the Lamb of God, and the first disciples follow Him as the recognized Messiah (i. 41), Him of whom Moses and the prophets wrote (i. 45), the Son of God, the King of Israel. No doubt the Fourth Evangelist believed that such recognition must have taken place, but if he knew Mark he can hardly have been unaware that he was contradicting him. The possibility should at least be considered that he was composing an original account, the product of his own faith working on the floating traditions of the Christian Church and uninfluenced by other accounts which gained currency simultaneously in quite different circles of believers.

St John does not forget the importance of the contrast he seeks to draw between Jesus and the Baptist. In chapter iii. 22–30 we read of a second testimony of John to Jesus. John was baptizing at Aenon, near Salim, and Jesus began also to baptize. The evangelist remarks (unless the words are a gloss) that John was not yet cast into prison, clearly implying that the ministries of Jesus and of John overlapped. His intention here may be to put Jesus and John side by side, but he certainly contradicts St Mark, who dates the beginning of the ministry of Jesus from the time that John was imprisoned by Herod (Mk. i. 14). Surely the simplest explanation is that the Fourth Evangelist was writing at a time when the acceptance of St Mark's Gospel had not yet fixed his tradition on the Church.

Yet this passage is one of those to which critics point as

presupposing a knowledge of the synoptic account. The evangelist is said to assume that the reader will know that John preached and drew great crowds whom he baptized, although John's work as a baptizer has been passed over in chapter i. His imprisonment is also mentioned incidentally, and no explanation is offered.[1] The argument is particularly weak. John was writing for Christians, and every Christian in the first century must have heard of the Baptist. That he had drawn crowds to his baptism must have been part of the common tradition, and so too was the fact that he had been imprisoned and executed by Herod. The assumption that such facts can only have been known to Christians who had read the Synoptic Gospels is gratuitous and misleading; and although the Fourth Evangelist refers to these facts, he does so in a manner inconsistent with the synoptic picture. At a time when Mark (or Mark and Luke) was known in the churches an evangelist could hardly have represented Jesus and John as excercising their ministries simultaneously; such a departure from the synoptic scheme would at once have been recognized and an explanation demanded. On the other hand, the Johannine account, even though unhistorical, would pass unchallenged at an earlier period in which traditions were still fragmentary and vague.

In only two other passages[2] is the Baptist mentioned, and these passages contribute nothing to the solution of our problem. Both are concerned with the significance of John's witness to Jesus, and the latter emphasizes his inferiority inasmuch as 'he did no sign'.

---

[1] Goguel, *Introduction au Nouveau Testament*, II, 217.
[2] Jn. v. 33, x. 41.

To sum up, we may conclude that there is little or no positive evidence that the author of the Fourth Gospel had read the synoptic accounts of the ministry of the Baptist, and there are many features of his narrative, of which, although some may be explained by the influence of dogmatic interest, the majority are most easily accounted for on the theory that he did not know any of the Synoptic Gospels. If he had read them, he held them in very low esteem.

Chapter II

JOHN II–IV

John ii. 1–11

LITTLE NEED be said about the account of the Marriage
Feast at Cana. We do not know the source of John's
information, and critics are not agreed as to the character
and significance of the story. It is regarded by the
evangelist as a manifestation of the glory of Jesus and as
a stimulus to the disciples' faith, but those critics are
probably right who consider its origin to be an allegory.[1]
The only point of contact with the synoptic tradition is
in the mention of the Mother of Jesus, and this is classed
by some (e.g. Goguel) among those passages in which a
knowledge of the Synoptic Gospels is assumed. Are we
to suppose then that Christians who had not read Matthew
or Luke thought that Jesus had no mother? So far as we
can judge, traditions about the family of Jesus were
meagre, but all Christians must have known that Mary
was His Mother, and the fact that she appears in a
Johannine story is no proof that the author had read one
or more of the other Gospels. Moreover, if we accept the
theory that there is an allegory behind the narrative, the
Mother of Jesus may not be Mary at all, but the Jewish
or Jewish Christian Church. She is not called Mary in
this passage.

John ii. 12

At length Jesus comes to Capernaum, where He remains
'not many days'. The statement may be said to summarize

---

[1] E.g. Loisy, *Le Quatrième Évangile*, pp. 139 ff.

traditions elaborated in the early chapters of Mark; but why should John mention His Mother and His brethren? They do not appear in Mark until chapter iii. 21 and 31, and then as critics rather than as admirers. John is nearer to synoptic tradition in chapter vii. 5, where we read: 'For neither did his brethren believe on him.' But the whole section (vii. 5–10) in which the brethren urge Jesus to go to Jerusalem in order that His disciples also may see the works which He does is certainly not reminiscent of anything in the Synoptic Gospels.[1] Indeed it reflects a point of view characteristic of the Fourth Gospel, the author of which clearly regards Jerusalem as the proper scene of the activites of the Christ and Galilee as a district in which Jesus walked for brief periods when retirement from Judaea was made necessary by the hostility of the Jews. It is difficult to believe that any Christian accustomed to read St Mark can have taken that view, however well it may have accorded with his own ideas of the dignity of the Christ. Even if it be granted that the evangelist's interest was not what we should call historical, and that he may have treated traditions with great freedom in developing his theme, yet it seems contrary to all canons of probability that he should have recast entirely the narrative of one or two written Gospels which had already secured enough acceptance to carry them round the world.

John ii. 13–22

This section relates an incident fully described by all the synoptic writers, and therefore from the point of view of

---

[1] See below, pp. 36 f.

our present enquiry it deserves careful scrutiny. According to John, Jesus goes up to Jerusalem because the Passover is near. There He finds merchants in the Temple and expels them. There follows a debate with the Jews as to His authority. In the Synoptic Gospels the cleansing of the Temple is placed during the last week before the crucifixion, and the resentment of the Sadducean authorities accounts in large measure for the arrest of Jesus (Mk. xi. 15–18).

Rejecting the theory that the Temple was twice cleansed, we are left with two alternatives; either the Fourth Evangelist so greatly preferred the earlier dating that he felt justified in disregarding (or rather in contradicting) the Marcan scheme, or he knew of a tradition that Christ had driven out the merchants from the Temple courts, but was acquainted with no written Gospel in which the incident was assigned a definite place in the history of the ministry. Before deciding between these alternatives it is worth while to compare in detail the several narratives and to consider whether the account of the Fourth Evangelist leaves a general impression of acquaintance with Mark, Matthew, or Luke.

All the Gospels are agreed that the incident occurred shortly before a Jewish Passover, when the merchants would find their trade most brisk. Mark speaks of those that sold and those that bought in the Temple, and John has the same word—τοὺς πωλοῦντας. Mark mentions 'the tables of the money-changers', τὰς τραπέζας τῶν κολλυβιστῶν, and John says that 'he poured out the gains of the money-changers and upset their tables'. Mark refers to the 'seats of them that sold doves', and

John mentions doves as part of the merchandise; verse 16 records that 'he said to the dove-sellers, Take these things hence'.

These similarities should certainly be noted, for they require to be explained. But are they so numerous and so close as to demand a theory of literary dependence? Whenever the story was told there must have been mention of 'sellers', 'tables', 'money-changers', and 'doves', for it could hardly have been related at all without the use of these words. On the other hand, the peculiar elements in the Johannine version deserve more notice than they generally receive. The Fourth Evangelist alone speaks of 'oxen and sheep'; he alone has the word κερματιστής for money-changer, though he uses κολλυβιστής in the next verse; he alone mentions the scourge of small cords. Whereas Mark says that Jesus turned over (κατέστρεψεν) the tables of the money-changers and the seats of them that sold doves, John says that He overturned (ἀνέτρεψεν) the tables of the money-changers and poured out their money. The Synoptists all represent Jesus as quoting Is. lvi. 7, 'My house shall be called a house of prayer for all nations', and adding, 'But ye have made it a den of robbers' (Jer. vii. 11); John only says that Jesus exclaimed: 'Take these things hence! Make not my Father's house a house of merchandise.' Then the disciples remember a quotation from the Scriptures, but it comes from Ps. lxix, not from Is. lvi, 'The zeal of thine house shall eat me up', a text much less appropriate than that which appears in the Synoptists. The cumulative effect of these contrasts is enough to throw considerable doubt on the assumption that John must have had the account of one or more of our Synoptic Gospels in mind.[1]

The sequel in the Fourth Gospel is of course wholly different from that in Mark. 'The Jews' demand a sign in proof of Jesus' authority, and Jesus answers, 'Destroy this temple, and in three days I will raise it up', a reference, as the evangelist points out, to the resurrection. It is interesting to compare the synoptic account of the demand for a sign. In Mk. viii. 11, 12 the Pharisees seek from Him a sign from Heaven, tempting Him, and the request is sternly refused; 'Why does this generation seek for a sign? Verily I say, no sign shall be given to this generation.' But this refusal did not suit Christian apologetic which saw signs in the miracles and in the resurrection, signs which only wilful perversity could refuse to recognize. So in the corresponding section of Matthew (xvi. 4) we read, 'An evil and adulterous generation seeketh after a sign, and no sign shall be given it save the sign of Jonah', and again in xii. 39, founded on a Q passage, the same words are expanded, 'For as Jonah was in the belly of the whale three days and three nights, so shall the Son of Man be three days and three nights in the heart of the earth', though Lk. xi. 30 gives quite another interpretation.

[1] Streeter suggests (*Four Gospels*, pp. 416ff.) that the author of the Fourth Gospel may have been an occasional pilgrim to Jerusalem, where he picked up scraps of Christian tradition, such as the story of Jesus' cleansing the Temple at the Passover season. 'Exact chronology is not a matter in regard to which popular local tradition is apt to be concerned', so the author may well have connected the incident with the wrong Passover. This is very probable, but not after Mark's arrangement of the incident had won general acceptance. Moreover, if John went up to the Temple his visits must have been before A.D. 70, and therefore he collected his material, and perhaps wrote his Gospel, before the Gospel of St Mark appeared!

The Fourth Evangelist, like Matthew, regards the resurrection as the great 'sign', but he introduces the idea in a manner which is in no way reminiscent of the Synoptic Gospels. His connecting of it with the well-known saying about the destruction of the Temple (Mk. xiv. 58, xv. 29) is an original feature which certainly does not suggest acquaintance with Matthew or Mark. John knew that a sign had been demanded from Jesus; so much he may have derived from oral tradition, and no doubt like St Matthew and the majority of Christians he regarded the resurrection as just such a sign. He also knew that Jesus had spoken of destroying the Temple and restoring it in three days, a saying for which there is ample evidence although it is not actually recorded in the Synoptic Gospels.[1] He interpreted it with reference to the resurrection, and what more natural than that he should connect it with the demand for a sign? Moreover, since the character of the Temple was here in question, it is a most suitable place to introduce the saying and the interpretation. But would it have been equally natural if the evangelist had been writing with Mark before him?

Without laying any stress on the point, we may notice in passing the theory of Loisy that the 'forty and six years' mentioned in verse 20 has reference to the age of Jesus, rather than to the time of building Herod's Temple, and therefore John thinks of Jesus as forty-six years old at this time (cp. viii. 57, 'Thou art not yet fifty years old'). If so, then we have a flat contradiction of Matthew and Luke without any obvious justification, for the Scriptural references are fanciful.[2]

---

[1] Mk. xiv. 58; *The Gospel of Peter*, §vii; Acts vi. 14.
[2] Loisy, *op. cit.* p. 151. Cp. Dan. ix. 25–27.

John ii. 23–25

The Resurrection was the great sign, but it was by no means the only one, and indeed the whole life of Jesus was a sign. So in these verses, 'As he was in Jerusalem at the Passover, at the feast, many believed on his name when they saw his signs which he did'. No doubt 'signs' means primarily 'miracles', and John develops an idea which influenced the Synoptists. But he betrays no knowledge of the quite definite disclaimer of Jesus which survives in Mk. viii. 12, and throughout the Fourth Gospel appeal is made to such 'signs' as Mark tells us that Jesus had declined to furnish. Can John have mislaid his 'copy of Mark'?[1]

John iii. 1–21

The problem of the identity of Nicodemus has troubled many commentators. He does not appear in the Synoptic Gospels, but he enjoys some prominence in St John, where he not only engages Jesus in the conversation recorded in chapter iii, but also, by defending Jesus to the chief priests and Pharisees in chapter vii, brings upon himself the scornful question, 'Art thou also of Galilee?' In chapter xix he reappears as the assistant of Joseph of Arimathea.

When we consider the difficulty of finding room for this prominent Pharisaic sympathizer in the synoptic scheme we cannot wonder that many critics find in Nicodemus an ideal figure. Bacon suggests that his name is 'a transliteration of the Naq Dimon of Talmudic

[1] Streeter's phrase.

tradition, celebrated for his wealth, and for having provided at his own expense baths for purifying pilgrims to the Temple', and further that his figure is composite, created from those of the Young Ruler, the Scribe who questioned Jesus as to the first commandment of the law, and Joseph of Arimathea.[1] If this latter theory is accepted it is surely more probable that such an amalgamation took place during the stage of oral tradition than that the Fourth Evangelist deliberately combined features drawn from well-known persons familiar in written narratives. So long as stories are passing from mouth to mouth almost anything may happen to the characters who figure in them, but when once tradition has been fixed in accepted writings confusion and serious modification are much less likely to occur.

The discourse to Nicodemus and the meditation thereon have so little in common with anything contained in the Synoptic Gospels that they hardly bear on the subject which we are discussing. All that can be said is that ideas which occur in the other Gospels (baptism with holy spirit, perfection, conditions of entry into the Kingdom) are here translated into Johannine language and fitted into the Johannine scheme.

John iv. 1–42

Few would find in the narrative of the brief ministry in Samaria of chapter iv any reference to synoptic tradition, much less to the Synoptic Gospels; but Bacon says: 'In John iv the Lucan substitute of a ministry among *Samaritans* is followed in preference to the Marcan story of the Syro-

---

[1] Bacon, *op. cit.* p. 368, note 2.

Phoenician woman.' This seems arbitrary. No doubt the
chapter is founded on a tradition that Jesus manifested
sympathy with some who were not Jews, and Luke and
John share a belief that Jesus actually passed through
Samaria, but there is here no positive evidence of a knowledge of the Third Gospel. Indeed it is difficult to think
that anyone brought up in the tradition embodied in our
Synoptic Gospels could have represented Jesus, thus early
in the ministry, proclaiming to a Samaritan woman that
He was the Messiah, which is the climax of the Johannine
account (iv. 26).

Verses 35–38: 'Say ye not that it is yet four months to
the harvest? Behold I say unto you, Lift up your eyes
and look on the fields because they are white unto
harvest, etc.', contain an echo of the saying recorded in
Mt. ix. 37 and Lk. x. 2: 'The harvest truly is plenteous,
but the labourers are few; pray ye therefore the Lord of
the Harvest that he may send labourers into his harvest.'
In Matthew the words are elicited by the sight of the
crowds 'as sheep without a shepherd', but in Luke they
are part of the charge to the Seventy, which is an indication that they were contained in Q without historical
context. This therefore was a current saying of Jesus of
which the synoptic writers availed themselves as best they
could. It is reasonable to suppose that the Fourth Evangelist did the same. He applies similar words to the
Samaritans, typical maybe of non-Jewish believers in
Jesus, but there is nothing whatever in his use of the
saying to suggest that he remembered how it had been
used by Matthew or Luke, or even that he knew Q. The
obscure verses which follow suggest, as Macgregor say

that we have here a 'conglomerate' passage composed of sayings originally uttered on various occasions, and subsequently brought together on account of their similarity of subject, in this case sowing and reaping.[1] Once again, it is much more probable that the materials for such a conglomeration would be drawn from floating traditions than from written Gospels in which the sayings already appeared in a definite context. It is not easy to find room for the Samaritan mission (verses 39–42) in the synoptic scheme, although it is said to have lasted only two days, and the suggestion that we have here an anticipation of the mission to Samaria described in Acts viii is not to be summarily rejected. The leader of that expedition was Philip, and the Fourth Evangelist has evidently drawn on a collection of traditions in which Philip was prominent.[2] This point, however, does not bear immediately on our present enquiry.

John iv. 43–45

These verses are very significant, whatever their precise position should be in the text. 'After two days Jesus went forth from thence into Galilee; for he himself bare witness that a prophet hath not honour in his own country. When therefore he came into Galilee, the Galileans received him, because they had seen all the things that he did in Jerusalem, for they too came to the feast.' In Mk. vi. 4 we read: 'Jesus said unto them, A prophet is not without honour save in his own country and among his own kin

---

[1] Macgregor, *Gospel of John*, p. 110.
[2] Jn. i. 43f., vi. 5, xii. 21, xiv. 8. A confusion between Philip the Apostle and Philip the Evangelist is more than probable.

and in his house.' Here, we are told, is a clear case of John's quoting from Mark. On the contrary, it is very nearly a clear proof that he did not know our Second Gospel. According to the synoptic account,[1] Jesus, after a successful ministry in Capernaum, journeys to Nazareth where He had been brought up, and there He is met with opposition and unbelief. Most appropriately He quotes the proverb to the effect that a prophet is never so regarded in his own πατρίς. The people of Nazareth knew Jesus too well as a carpenter to receive Him as a prophet. John's outlook is wholly different. He thinks of Judaea as the πατρίς of the Christ, and uses the proverb, which tradition said had been quoted by Jesus, not to account for His rejection at Nazareth, but to explain the indifference of the people of Judaea. There is no reason for supposing that the evangelist had read Mk. vi. 4. Even the 'quotation' is not accurate:

Mk. vi. 4: Οὐκ ἔστιν προφήτης ἄτιμος εἰ μὴ ἐν τῇ πατρίδι αὐτοῦ κ.τ.λ.

Jn. iv. 44: Προφήτης ἐν τῇ ἰδίᾳ πατρίδι τιμὴν οὐκ ἔχει.

John knew that Jesus had used some such words, but he did not know in what connexion they had been spoken.

This conclusion is supported in the next verse where we read that the Galileans received Him because they had seen what He had done at Jerusalem at the feast. Is it credible that the writer can have had at the back of his mind any such picture as that presented by Mark and Luke, who place the ministry of Jesus almost wholly in Galilee? If John knew our Second and Third Gospels

---

[1] Luke alters the order of events for reasons of his own.

then he contradicted them deliberately for dogmatic reasons, but it is much more probable that he did not know them.

John iv. 46–54

In these verses is related the healing of the nobleman's son. Jesus came to Cana of Galilee, and while He was there a certain nobleman, whose son was sick at Capernaum, hearing that Jesus was paying one of His rare visits to Galilee, came and besought Him to heal his son. After a brief conversation on the subject of 'believing' Jesus declared 'Thy son liveth'. The man 'believed', and as he was returning to Capernaum his servants met him with the news that his son was cured. On enquiry he found that the boy began to amend from the moment that Jesus had spoken the words 'Thy son liveth'. He himself 'believed' and his whole house. 'This was the second sign wrought by Jesus when he was come from Judaea into Galilee.'

The close similarity of this story to that of the healing of the centurion's servant, narrated by Matthew and Luke, has long been noticed. In the synoptic accounts a centurion at Capernaum[1] appeals to Jesus on behalf of his servant (Mt. παῖς, Lk. δοῦλος). According to Matthew Jesus proposes to go and heal him, whereupon the centurion answers: 'Lord I am not worthy that thou shouldest come under my roof, but speak the word only, and my servant will be healed.' Jesus commends the man's faith in high terms, 'Verily I say unto you, I have not found so great faith in Israel'; and he grants the

---

[1] But what was a Roman officer doing in the dominions of Antipas? John's βασιλικός is more likely to be original. D has βασιλίσκος.

request, so that the servant is healed *in that very hour* (Mt. viii. 5–13). Luke's variations are considerable, so considerable that it is doubtful whether he was using the same source. According to the Third Gospel the centurion sent to Jesus an embassy who spoke well of his piety, and when Jesus was approaching the house he sent another embassy of his friends to entreat Jesus not to trouble to come under his unworthy roof. The rest of the conversation is close to Matthew's version, so that Luke's earlier alterations may be deliberate (Lk. vii. 1–10).[1]

In outline this story resembles the Johannine narrative very closely. A person of importance at Capernaum had a son or servant[2] who was seriously ill. He appealed to Jesus who healed him from a distance by the word of power and who spoke of the man's faith, either frankly commending it, as in the Synoptists, or raising the question of the foundation of faith in general, as in the Fourth Gospel. Few critics will deny that it is the same tradition that appears in all the Gospels, and we are presented with different 'paradigms' on the theme of faith. But if so, we must conclude either that St John has treated the synoptic narrative with something like contempt, or that the tradition which he worked into his Gospel did not reach him in the same form as that which appears in either Matthew or Luke. The latter hypothesis seems obviously preferable. When the Fourth Evangelist wrote his Gospel a story was current of Jesus' having cured the son of a well-to-do man at Capernaum, and this story

---

[1] Creed, *St Luke, ad loc.*
[2] The ambiguity of the word παῖς would account for the variations in the tradition.

was often quoted both as an example of the power of Jesus to heal at a distance and as an illustration of faith, which to the Fourth Evangelist meant belief in Jesus as the Son of God. But there is no hint that he was in any way influenced by his recollections of Matthew or Luke. Indeed it is doubtful whether he would have recognized the story of the centurion as identical with his own story of the nobleman.[1]

We could hardly have a better illustration of the state of tradition in the Christian churches when the Fourth Gospel was written. Stories about Jesus had long been current, and they were used to illustrate points of doctrine; but by now they had diverged so widely that different versions of one tradition were hardly recognizable as referring to the same event. As yet no particular version had been stereotyped by the acceptance of written Gospels.

---

[1] Even Streeter allows that John's is 'a version preserved in a different line of tradition'. The phrase accurately describes many other passages.

Chapter III

JOHN V–X

John v. 1–9

CHAPTER V opens with the miracle of the healing of the impotent man at the pool of Bethzatha, a story which has no obvious parallel in the Synoptic Gospels. Professor Bacon called Jn. v 'a recasting of Mk. ii. 1–iii. 6 in our evangelist's characteristic manner'.[1] But that is to beg the question. It is true that the Marcan chapters contain the record of miracles, and a dispute about the Sabbath, but it needs an active, perhaps an uncontrolled, imagination to see in the Johannine account a conscious rewriting of the plain narrative of the Second Gospel. It may be that Christian tradition turned the paralytic of Capernaum into an impotent man in Jerusalem;[2] but, if so, the change was surely made by ill-informed teachers and not by a writer who had the work of earlier evangelists before him. Here again the simpler hypothesis is to be preferred; the Fourth Evangelist has taken a story familiar in oral tradition, worked it up, and used it for his own purpose. We may note that his purpose is not by any means the same as that of the Synoptists in telling the story of the paralytic; for them the point at issue is the power of the Son of Man, by whom they mean Jesus, to forgive sins; but Jn. v. 1–9 leads to the sabbath controversy. The Fourth

---

[1] Bacon, *op. cit.* p. 377.
[2] We may compare the transference of post-resurrection appearances from Galilee to Jerusalem, as in Luke and John. But it is very unlikely that this was the deliberate work of the evangelists.

Evangelist knew that Jesus fell out with the Jewish leaders on the question of healing on the Sabbath, and he wished to include teaching of great importance in his account of the controversy; so he took a current story and used it as an introduction to theological debate. The story itself is no doubt regarded as the record of 'a sign', and it is related in such a manner as to bring out fully its miraculous features, but there is nothing to suggest that the evangelist was 'rewriting' Mark's account of the miracle at Capernaum. The details are entirely different except the words Ἔγειρε ἆρον τὸν κράβαττόν σου καὶ περιπάτει, which occur also in Mk. ii. 9.

How much weight can be put on this solitary correspondence? Wherever a story was told of Jesus' having cured an impotent man the words of power would be quoted, and a sentence of seven words would not impose any great tax on the memory. Both Mark and John use the vulgar word κράβαττος because at an early stage the original Aramaic had been so translated, and the whole phrase passed into Christian tradition. But when we observe how widely the two accounts differ in other respects it seems hazardous to assume literary dependence on the evidence of a single phrase.[1]

If the Fourth Evangelist had Mark in mind, why did he represent the Jews as objecting to the man's carrying his bed? There is no hint of any such objection in the

[1] It is surprising that Streeter should have laid so much stress on the use of this phrase, and have spoken of the 'vocabulary of Mark' as probably familiar to John (*op. cit.* p. 398). It was rather the vocabulary of the early Church that was familiar to John, and he had not the nice discrimination of Matthew and Luke, who rejected κράβαττος.

synoptists, and Mark does not make the healing of the
paralytic the occasion of controversy about the Sabbath.
It may be, as Bacon held, that John's account combines
the features of several narratives which appear separately
in Mark; but once more, we must ask whether such con-
flation is more likely to have taken place during the stage
of oral transmission, or in the mind of a skilled writer who
had other documents to work on, documents in which
these incidents were entirely distinct.

In the rest of chapter v there seems to be nothing
reminiscent of the Synoptic Gospels; we may therefore
pass on to chapter vi.

John vi. 1–15

The feeding of the five thousand is the only miracle of
Jesus narrated in all four Gospels. Here then we have a
story which is to be identified without question with a
story contained in the Synoptic Gospels, and if our author
derived his knowledge of it from them the fact should
be unmistakably apparent. Even though, as Bacon says,
'transcription is not the method of the Fourth Evangelist',
he could hardly fail to betray the source of his knowledge,
and he would not be likely to introduce serious contradictions without sufficient reason. What do we find?

1. The introduction is quite different from that of
Mark. According to the Second Gospel the disciples
returned to Jesus after their missionary tour and reported
their success. Jesus replied, 'Come ye yourselves apart
into a desert place and rest awhile'. So they went away
in the boat into a desert place. But many saw them going,
and running together from all the cities the multitudes

arrived first at the place of landing. Jesus, touched by their need, began to teach them many things. When the evening was come the problem of food arose and Jesus worked the miracle to supply the material needs of those to whom he had already ministered spiritually. Mark's geography is vague, and it is not clear which shore of the lake he has in mind, but the mention of cities and multitudes seems to rule out the eastern side.

The Johannine account is hardly less vague, but if chapter vi should follow immediately after chapter iv, as seems probable, Jesus is thought of as coming down from Cana of Galilee by the road which approaches the lake near Tiberias. He crosses the water, but in what direction is not stated; only we are told that another voyage was necessary in the evening to reach Capernaum (vi. 17). Crowds follow Him because they have seen the signs wrought upon the sick, although no such cures have been described. Jesus therefore goes into 'the mountain', and sits there with His disciples. John has not derived this picture from Mk. vi, for the Second Evangelist thinks of a level place near the shore.

It has been noted that Matthew places the feeding of the four thousand on a hill (Mt. xv. 29), and he says that Jesus sat down, but since few allege that John was indebted to Matthew, it follows that the details were derived from oral tradition which would certainly assimilate the two stories. Surely the same explanation may be given of other details. It is gratuitous to suppose with Macgregor that the words ἐπάρας οὖν τοὺς ὀφθαλμοὺς ὁ Ἰησοῦς are an echo of Lk. vi. 20: καὶ αὐτὸς ἐπάρας τοὺς ὀφθαλμοὺς αὐτοῦ εἰς τοὺς μαθητὰς αὐτοῦ. The phrase is natural

enough as an introduction to what follows and may well
have belonged to current Christian phraseology. Why
should John take it from an entirely different context in
a written source? He omits any mention of the com-
passion of Jesus, of His healings,[1] and of the teaching
which is an essential feature of the Marcan account.

2. John's conception of what happened is quite different from that of Mark. The omission of the teaching
which in the Synoptists precedes the miracle might be
thought to have been deliberate, inasmuch as John intends
to give a long account of the teaching which follows; but
it alters the picture entirely. In Mark the crowds are fed
because they have lingered too long listening to the words
of Jesus, and the proposal of the disciples that they should
go into the country and villages round about to buy food
is rejected by Jesus. John has no such thought. He
supposes the sign to have been given in the afternoon
(vi. 16), and he represents Jesus as proceeding at once,
without apparent need, to work the miracle. The evangelist's mind is fixed exclusively on the question of the
feeding of the multitude, and there is no realistic
setting.

3. John's account of the miracle differs in almost every
possible way from that of Mark. In Mark the disciples
intervene with the suggestion that Jesus should send the
multitudes away while there is yet time for them to buy

[1] Mt. xiv. 14, Lk. ix. 11. Streeter compares Jn. vi. 2 with its
mention of healings immediately before the miracle with these
passages. But John does not seem to mean that the healings took
place after Jesus had crossed the lake, they only explain why the
crowd followed Him. This point tells rather against the theory of
dependence.

food, and it is only when Jesus replies 'Give ye them to eat' that they answer 'Shall we go and buy two hundred pennyworth of bread and give them to eat?' Jesus ignores the implied rebuke, and asks how many loaves they have. After enquiry, they reply 'Five, and two fishes (δύο ἰχθύας)'. In John, Jesus assumes the need of feeding the great crowd and initiates the conversation with Philip, 'Whence shall we buy bread that these may eat?' Philip replies, 'Two hundred pennyworth of bread are not sufficient for them that each may take a little'. Then Andrew breaks in with the remark, 'There is a lad here who hath five barley loaves and two small fishes (ὀψάρια), but what are they among so many?'

It may be claimed with some confidence that this is a completely independent account. The words used are different, the speakers are different, the only point of contact is in the single phrase διακοσίων δηναρίων ἄρτοι, and even that is accusative in Mark and nominative in John.

But it is said that the inclusion of an identical phrase 'can hardly be accidental'.[1] That depends on what is meant by 'accidental'. If it means that two writers composing an account of an event which had never been heard of before 'accidentally' hit upon the same phrase, that would indeed be astonishing. But if it means that two writers telling a story which had been familiar to Christians for at least a generation both included one striking phrase such as would probably be always used when the story was related, then we have the kind of 'accident' which was almost certain to occur. 'Two

---

[1] Streeter, *op. cit.* p. 397.

hundred pennyworth of bread' is just the kind of phrase likely to linger in the popular memory. True, it is omitted by Matthew and Luke, evidently because they did not like the tone of the disciples' answer to Jesus in which it is included by Mark; but John brings in the words quite naturally in Philip's reply to Jesus' question. There is no suggestion here of a rebuke to Jesus, and so John is able to preserve a traditional feature of the story.

It is surprising in the highest degree that here, as elsewhere, critics should lay so much emphasis on a trivial agreement between John and Mark which can quite easily be explained as due to the influence of oral tradition, and ignore almost entirely the heavy weight of evidence which goes to shew that John was not familar with the Marcan account.

It is hardly less surprising that until recently critics have been accustomed to give so little attention to the influence of oral tradition. It seems to have been tacitly assumed that the evangelists wrote in a kind of vacuum in which the Church had been content to live for half a century. It is to be hoped that *Formgeschichte* will finally deliver us from this delusion.[1]

4. The description of the meal is no closer to John's supposed source. According to Mark, Jesus commanded ἀνακλιθῆναι πάντας συμπόσια συμπόσια ἐπὶ τῷ χλωρῷ χόρτῳ, and all the Synoptists use some compound of κλίνω.

---

[1] Professor Cadbury writes: 'Form Criticism carries the mind back to the stage before the written relationship, the stage between Jesus and the Gospels, and by staking out its claims in that field, by indicating its existence and formative importance, the new school of criticism has performed already a distinct service': *Quantulacumque*, p. 100.

John mentions the grass, but in a different way, 'There was much grass in that place', and he renders the command of Jesus ποιήσατε τοὺς ἀνθρώπους ἀναπεσεῖν. He says that Jesus *took* the loaves and *gave thanks*. These are eucharistic phrases, which adequately accounts for their use; but all the Synoptists have εὐλόγησεν as compared with John's εὐχαριστήσας,[1] and they add that he *brake* the bread. Mark and his copyists say that they were all filled (ἐχορτάσθησαν), John says ὡς δὲ ἐνεπλήσθησαν. According to John it is Jesus who commands the disciples to collect the fragments that remain lest anything be wasted, and the evangelist emphasizes the fact that the twelve baskets-full remained out of the five barley loaves; on the other hand, Matthew and Mark lay stress on the number of the participants in the meal. These are trivial points of difference, but taken together they do not strengthen the case for literary dependence. Finally, John describes the effect of the sign upon the multitude who had eaten, and adds that, convinced that He was 'the Prophet who cometh into the world', they wished to seize Him to make Him King; but Jesus withdrew again into the mountain alone—to escape the multitude, not, as in Mark, to pray.[2]

If it were not that critics had been unconsciously influenced by the assumption that since John's is the latest Gospel he must have known the work of the earlier

[1] In the account of the four thousand εὐχαριστήσας is substituted for εὐλόγησεν, another example of the influence of oral tradition.

[2] Streeter remarks that trifling and obvious modifications of Mark's account of the Five Thousand suggest that in John recollection of the details from one miracle had become confused with the other (*op. cit.* p. 413). Again, just the kind of assimilation that takes place in *oral* traditions.

evangelists, they would surely have recognized here an independent account. A close study of the four Gospels suggests that John knew a popular story, a story probably familiar to all Christians at the time when he wrote, but there is no evidence to prove that he had read it in Mark or Luke and considerable reason for concluding that he had not.

John vi. 16–21

Like the Synoptists, John tells of Jesus' walking on the sea immediately after the feeding of the five thousand. If the two miracles were entirely disconnected the juxtaposition might be significant; but they go well together, and they were no doubt associated in oral tradition. The miraculous meal had taken place somewhere over the water, and therefore the disciples had to return in the boat to their own district. Given a tradition that Jesus had come to them while they were on the water, this was a very good place to insert the miracle, and we cannot doubt that it was here recorded from an early date. Even though the incident cannot be regarded as historical, being in fact another version of the story of the risen Christ approaching His disciples by the Lake of Galilee (Jn. xxi), yet owing to the strange instability of the latter incident in early tradition, as proved by its disappearance from the First and Third Gospels, it was necessary to find another context for it in the traditions of the ministry.

John here has not much in common with the Synoptists. He mentions Capernaum as the destination of the disciples, whereas Mark has Bethsaida.[1] Mark says that Jesus compelled His disciples to precede Him to the other

---

[1] Although in vi. 53 John says that they moored at Gennesaret.

side 'while he sent away the crowd'; but according to John, Jesus had retired alone into the mountain. John's description of the storm owes nothing to Mark:

Mk. vi. 47. The boat was in the midst of the sea, and he alone upon the land. And seeing them distressed in rowing, for the wind was contrary to them, about the fourth watch of the night he cometh to them, walking upon the sea.

Jn. vi. 17. And it had now grown dark, and Jesus had not yet come unto them. And the sea grew rough, for a great wind was blowing. Therefore when they had rowed twenty-five or thirty furlongs they see Jesus walking upon the sea and coming near the boat.

There is hardly a word in John's account that is reminiscent of Mark except the mention of rowing, and the phrase περιπατοῦντα ἐπὶ τῆς θαλάσσης, a phrase which must surely have been stereotyped wherever the story was told. On the other hand, the Fourth Evangelist mentions distance where Mark speaks of time, and he says that the wind was strong, whereas Mark says that it was contrary. Mark says also that when the disciples saw Jesus they thought He was a spirit and cried out in terror; John merely states that they were afraid, and it is only in recording the words of Jesus (Ἐγώ εἰμι, μὴ φοβεῖσθε) that he agrees verbally with the Second Evangelist. It is just such short sayings of Jesus that would become fixed in tradition,[1] and even here John omits Mark's θαρσεῖτε. In the concluding sentence John is quite independent:

Mk. vi. 51. And he went up into the boat, and the wind ceased.

Jn. vi. 21. Therefore they wished to take him into the

[1] 'Epigrams easily circulate by word of mouth': Streeter, *op. cit.* p. 409.

boat, and immediately the boat came to the land to which they were going.

Why this alteration if it was from Mark that John derived the story? If it be said that he was influenced by other versions of the story, may we not conclude that such other versions are a sufficient basis for his narrative?

The discourse which follows is in many ways of great importance, but it seems to throw little light upon our immediate subject. Most critics admit that it contains the evangelist's contribution to the Church's doctrine of the Eucharist, and that its place here and not after the Last Supper is due to St John's deliberate intention to correct some current ideas of which he disapproved. But few elements in the discourse have any real parallels in the Synoptic Gospels. One verse has a familiar ring: 'The Jews said, Is this not Jesus, the son of Joseph, whose father and mother we know?' which is reminiscent of Mk. vi. 3: 'Is not this the carpenter, the son of Mary, and the brother of James and Joses and Jude and Simon?' But the verbal correspondence is not close, and the context is entirely different. John may well have known that the critics of Jesus had objected to His claims on the ground that His family was known, and he used the tradition in what seemed to him a suitable setting; but there is certainly no indication that he was familiar with Mark's account of the scene in the synagogue at Nazareth.

John vi. 66–71

In these verses we have, so it is said, the Johannine equivalent of Peter's great confession in Mk. viii. 27–33. In a sense no doubt that is true. The words, 'Thou hast

words of eternal life, and we have believed and known
that thou art the Holy One of God', sum up the Johannine
conception of Jesus as the source of life eternal which
takes the place of the synoptic faith in Jesus the Messiah.
But to say that these verses represent 'a rewriting of the
Marcan account' is to go far beyond the evidence. The
only real point of contact is the belief that Peter understood the Lord's Person best, and that was probably the
conviction of the early Church. Again, although the
phrase 'the Holy One of God' is Marcan, Mark puts it
into the mouth of a demoniac, a fact which would not
commend it to the Fourth Evangelist. Lastly, the reference to Judas at the end of the discourse may be
significant in view of the synoptic references to Judas at
the Last Supper. But at the most it indicates that John
had the current accounts of the Last Supper at the back
of his mind when he composed this discourse, it does not
prove literary dependence on any one of our Gospels. It
may be, and probably is, quite accidental.

John vii. 1–13

Chapter vii opens with the statement that 'After this
Jesus walked in Galilee, for he would not walk in Judaea,
because the Jews sought to kill him'. Again we note the
assumption that Judaea was His proper sphere, and that
His visits to Galilee were exceptional. This is no proof
that John had not read the Synoptic Gospels, but if he
knew them, he had no regard for their authority. Nothing
could be further from synoptic tradition than the conversation with the Lord's brethren. 'They said therefore
unto him, Depart hence and go into Judaea in order that

thy disciples also may see the works which thou doest; for no man worketh anything in secret and himself seeketh to be known openly; since thou doest these things, manifest thyself to the world. For neither did his brethren believe on him.' The sole point of contact with Mark is to be found in the Marcan account of the attempt of οἱ παρ' αὐτοῦ to lay hold on Him, for they said that He was mad (Mk. iii. 21), and the visit of His mother and His brethren in Mk. iii. 31, which leads to the saying: 'Whosoever shall do the will of God, he is my brother and my sister and my mother.' A tradition of unbelief on the part of His family underlies both these passages, but that is all. For the rest, it would appear that the Fourth Evangelist thought of the disciples as resident in Judaea where alone they could see His works, and he supposed that Jesus could manifest Himself to the world only in Judaea. Wellhausen saw here a relic of an earlier tradition according to which Jesus had not yet visited Jerusalem; but how then could there be disciples in Judaea? It is rather another example of the evangelist's conviction that Galilee was a remote and unimportant district in which it was not proper for Jesus to remain. He did not derive this conviction from a study of the Synoptic Gospels. Unless his presentation is purely arbitrary, it must rest upon information derived from oral tradition which branched off from the main stream at quite an early period when stories had not yet been set in any general framework. No doubt subsequent development of Johannine tradition was very considerable, but it was for the most part independent development, alternative to that which found expression in the Synoptic Gospels.

John vii. 20

In the controversy with the Jews which follows the return
to Jerusalem the multitude answer: 'Thou hast a demon;
who seeketh to kill thee?' The nearest parallel is Mk. iii.
22: 'The Scribes who came down from Jerusalem said,
He hath Beezeboul, and by the Prince of the Demons he
casteth out the demons.' It would be a bold claim to say
that John is here dependent upon Mark. He knows that
Jesus was suspected of being possessed, but he betrays no
knowledge of the Marcan setting.

Similarly in the verses which follow (vii. 22, 23) the
argument is used that the Law itself allows the Sabbath
to be broken, which is reminiscent of the argument in
Matthew that the priests profane the Sabbath and are
guiltless (xii. 5). But there is no close correspondence,
and we can only say that there was a tradition that Jesus
had used some form of the *tu quoque* argument in controversy with the Jews about the Sabbath. The concluding
verses of the paragraph, 'Many of the multitude believed
on Him, and said, When the Christ shall come will he do
more signs than this man hath done?' are quite inconsistent
with the synoptic scheme.

John vii. 40–44

The passage records further debate as to the Person of
Jesus. 'Some of the multitude said, This is indeed the
prophet. Others said, This is the Christ. But others said,
Doth the Christ come out of Galilee? Hath not the
Scripture said that the Christ cometh of the seed of David
and from Bethlehem, the village where David was?

Therefore there was a division of the multitude because
of him.' Few would claim that these verses imply a
knowledge of Mk. viii. 27 and parallels. They raise the
very interesting question whether or not the Fourth
Evangelist knew the tradition embodied in the synoptic
birth-narratives that Jesus was born at Bethlehem. If he
did, he was content to allow his readers to answer the
objection of the multitudes for themselves. But it is
certainly surprising that although he is clearly aware of
Jewish objections to the claims of Jesus founded upon a
knowledge of His birth and origin (i. 46, vi. 42, vii. 27),
and he twice calls Jesus 'the son of Joseph', he never
answers these objections by denying that Joseph was the
father of Jesus or by asserting that Jesus was born at
Bethlehem. Nor does he ever call Jesus 'the Son of
David'. The most obvious explanation is that the Fourth
Evangelist wrote at a time and in a circle in which the
tradition that Jesus was born of the Virgin Mary at
Bethlehem, the city of David, had not yet become
established. If so, he did not know our Synoptic Gospels.[1]

The alternative explanation is that St John regarded
the earthly origin of Jesus as quite irrelevant to His claims.
The question belongs to a higher sphere into which the
Jews cannot enter: 'I know whence I came and whither
I go; but ye know not whence I come nor whither I go'

---

[1] Mark has no birth narrative, but he makes Bartimaeus cry 'Jesus,
thou Son of David', and he introduces the difficult debate concerning
the propriety of the use of the term (Mk. xii. 35). Perhaps when
Mark wrote the question had been raised, but the Church as a whole
had not decided how it was to be met. Mark represents an intermediate stage between the tradition underlying John, who knows
nothing about any claim that Jesus was the Son of David, and
Matthew who introduces the title on every possible occasion.

(viii. 14, ix. 29); His true Father is God whom the Jews do not know (viii. 19); only their stupidity could lead them to ask, Where is thy father? Even so, there is no hint of a knowledge of the synoptic birth-narratives, although viii. 41 may conceivably reflect the Jewish reaction to the preaching of the Virgin Birth. '*We* are not born of fornication, we have one Father, even God.' To which Jesus replies that the Jews are the children of the devil!

There is nothing more in the chapter which has any obvious bearing on our subject until we reach the last verse: 'Therefore they took up stones to cast on him; but Jesus hid himself and went out of the Temple.' There is here an echo of the tradition embodied in Lk. iv. 29 where the Jews in the synagogue at Nazareth led him to the brow of a hill that they might throw him down; 'but Jesus passed through the midst and went his way'. But every circumstance is different and there is no indication that John had read the Lucan passage.[1]

John ix

Chapter ix introduces the man blind from birth whom Jesus healed. Some critics regard him as a composite figure compounded of Bartimaeus and the blind man of Bethsaida in connexion with whose cure the use of spittle is recorded (Mk. viii. 22). It may be so, but again we must insist that there is no reason to suppose that John had *written* accounts in mind, such as those of Mk. viii and x. It is amongst oral traditions that confusion takes place. No doubt the narrative is largely if not wholly

[1] Cp. also Jn. x. 39.

symbolical, but even so, we have no right to assume that
the author has consciously taken such liberties with the
historical records as the theory of Bacon would demand.

John x

The parable of the Good Shepherd may well be a development of that of the Lost Sheep,[1] but there is nothing to
suggest that the Fourth Evangelist was acquainted with
the text of Mt. xviii or Lk. xv.

There is no need to insist on the exclusively 'Johannine'
character of the rest of the chapter. The Jews take up
stones to stone Him 'not for any good work, but for
blasphemy, because thou, being a man, makest thyself
God'. This charge takes the place of the objections to
messianic claims in the Synoptic Gospels, and we hear
nothing of the threat to the Temple, which has already
been turned into a prophecy of the resurrection (Jn. ii. 19).
The brief account of the ministry beyond Jordan, where
John was at first baptizing, cannot be fitted into the
Marcan scheme. Perhaps it is true that the fact would
not trouble the Fourth Evangelist. But perhaps he was
ignorant of the Marcan scheme.

[1] Macgregor says, 'The allegory awakens echoes of several passages
in the synoptics, e.g. Mt. vii. 13, ix. 36, xviii. 12, xxvi. 31' (*op. cit.*
p. 234). Distant echoes indeed!

Chapter IV

JOHN XI–XVII

John xi

THE LONG account of the raising of Lazarus marks the beginning of the Johannine passion narrative. In a sense the whole Gospel is a passion narrative, for the Fourth Evangelist has the great consummation always in mind; but from the beginning of chapter xi attention is concentrated on the circumstances which led to the arrest and trial of Jesus. It is no accident that fifty-three verses are devoted to a single incident. In the story of the raising of Lazarus St John sees the supreme manifestation of the divine power of Jesus whereby He is proclaimed the Resurrection and the Life, and this manifestation is enough to bring to a head the hostility of the Jews.

In several respects this chapter bears on our present enquiry. 1. Lazarus is described as 'from Bethany, of the village of Mary and Martha her sister'. 'We can say without doubt', writes Goguel, 'that John knew Luke', and he quotes this passage as clearly based upon Lk. x. 38 ff. Indeed, this is one of the two passages which he thinks puts literary dependence beyond question.[1] But is that true? It is only Luke of the Synoptists who mentions

---

[1] The other reference is to the High Priest Annas (Lk. iii. 2, Jn. xviii. 13, 24)! Of other contacts Goguel admits that 'Literary dependence is not certain here' and that 'a common trait is accompanied by too many elements of dissimilarity to make possible the thought of direct dependence'. (Goguel, *op. cit.* II, 221 f.) Then why does he say without hesitation that John knew Luke?

Martha and Mary among the women friends of Jesus, but unless we are to assume that no one of the early believers who had not read Luke could ever have heard of them there is no proof at all that the Fourth Evangelist derived his information from the Third Gospel. Indeed there are clear indications that he did not. St Luke does not tell us where he supposed that the sisters lived, but if we are to give any weight to the context the 'certain village' of Lk. x. 38 was in Galilee, and even John would have hesitated to identify it with Bethany, two miles from Jerusalem. Luke of course betrays no knowledge of Lazarus, the brother of Mary and Martha, and still less does he give any hint that Martha's sister had anointed the Lord with ointment and wiped His feet with her hair (Jn. xi. 2). The only woman mentioned by Luke who did anything of the kind was the sinner who followed Jesus into the house of Simon the Pharisee (Lk. vii. 38).

Critics[1] have appealed with so much confidence to this passage as proving that John knew Mark and Luke that it is worth while to set forth at some length the references in the four Gospels to Martha, Mary, and the women who ministered to Jesus while He sat at meat.

As to Martha and Mary, Luke says that in a certain village in Galilee a woman named Martha received Jesus into her house. She had a sister Mary who sat at Jesus' feet and heard His word. Martha was distracted by her domestic duties, and complained that Jesus was content to let Mary sit idle. Jesus gently rebuked her unnecessary preoccupation and commended Mary's choice of the good part (Lk. x. 38ff.).

[1] E.g. Streeter, *op. cit.* p. 402 f.

John says that Mary and Martha lived at Bethany with their brother Lazarus. Mary is apparently regarded as the elder sister, since she is named first here and alone in verse 45. This was the Mary who anointed the feet of Jesus.[1] The sisters send an appeal to Jesus to come and heal their brother, but when at last He comes Lazarus has been dead and buried four days. Martha goes out to meet Jesus while Mary sits at home. Shortly afterwards Mary is summoned secretly by Martha, and she too comes to Jesus. The Jews follow to the tomb to provide appropriate witnesses. The miracle follows, but we hear no more of the sisters (John xi).

In Lk. vii. 36ff. we read of a woman of the city who approached Jesus in the house of Simon the Pharisee in the early days of the ministry. She broke an alabaster box of ointment, and, standing behind by His feet and weeping, she began to sprinkle His feet with her tears and to wipe them with her hair, and she kissed His feet and anointed them with the ointment. Her devotion won the commendation of Jesus who contrasted her love with Simon's patronizing superiority: 'Her sins which are many are forgiven, for she loved much.' The story does not hang together well in some respects, but there we have Luke's version of the tradition that a woman had come to Jesus and ministered to Him at a feast. We may compare John. A supper is made at Bethany six days before the Passover. Martha serves, Lazarus sits at meat, and Mary anoints the feet of Jesus. John has here contacts with Mark and Matthew, who, although they do not mention Martha and

---

[1] Since her action is only described in the following chapter the words may be a gloss, but there is no doubt about the identification.

Mary, describe a meal at Bethany in the house of Simon the Leper and tell of a woman who anointed the head of Jesus (Mk. xiv. 3 ff., Mt. xxi. 6 ff.).

Let us note first those points in which the Fourth Evangelist might perhaps be thought to be dependent on one or other of the synoptic accounts.

1. He represents the meal as held at Bethany, as do Matthew and Mark. Luke omits.

2. He says that 'Martha served' (cp. Lk. x. 38 ff.).

3. He describes the action of a woman who·anointed the Lord with ointment (μύρον).

4. He uses Mark's exact phrase μύρου νάρδου πιστικῆς.

5. He uses the word πολυτίμου to describe its value, which is reminiscent of Mark's πολυτελοῦς and of Matthew's βαρυτίμου.

6. He records a protest that the ointment might have been sold and given to the poor, and he has Mark's phrase to describe its value τριακοσίων δηναρίων though he omits Mark's ἐπάνω, and transposes the words.

7. He records the reply of Jesus Ἄφες αὐτήν, which is very near to Mark's Ἄφετε αὐτήν.

8. He goes on to refer to the entombment (ἐνταφιασμός), of which the woman's action is in some sense anticipatory.

9. He quotes the saying τοὺς πτωχοὺς γὰρ πάντοτε ἔχετε μεθ' ἑαυτῶν ἐμὲ δὲ οὐ πάντοτε ἔχετε,[1] and his words are in almost exact agreement with Mark, although the latter interpolates a sentence ('and whensoever ye will ye can do them good') which does not appear in Matthew.

This is an impressive list, and we cannot wonder that critics who have an eye only for similarities declare that

---

[1] But the words are omitted by D Syr[sin] and Arm.

the passage proves the dependence of John on Mark, if not on Luke. But let us proceed to enumerate the differences between the several accounts.

1. John makes no mention of Simon the Leper, and he does not make it clear in whose house the feast was held, although, since Martha served, we may perhaps presume that the house was hers.

2. The mention of Lazarus explains the mediaeval identification of Lazarus with Simon, and hence the belief that Lazarus was a leper. Only on an uncritical view of the Gospels is the identification justified.

3. John says that it was Mary, sister of Martha, who anointed the Lord. This is not suggested in any of the synoptic accounts.

4. The amount of ointment implied by John is very large, a pound in weight. An ἀλάβαστρον strong enough to contain such a quantity could not have been crushed in a woman's hand (Mk. συντρίψασα).

5. John says that Mary anointed *the feet* of Jesus (ἤλειψεν τοὺς πόδας), whereas Mark has κατέχεεν αὐτοῦ τῆς κεφαλῆς, and she wiped His feet with her hair (ἐξέμαξεν ταῖς θριξὶν αὐτῆς τοὺς πόδας αὐτοῦ). We are reminded of Lk. vii. 38: καὶ ταῖς θριξὶν τῆς κεφαλῆς αὐτῆς ἐξέμασσεν.

6. According to John it is Judas who protests, not the τινες of Mark, nor the 'disciples' of Matthew.

The reply of Jesus according to John, though faintly reminiscent of the words recorded in Mark, has a totally different significance. According to Mark the woman has anticipated His burial, and the promise is given that her devotion shall not be forgotten. The words in John, though they have given much trouble to commentators

THE MEAL AT BETHANY

Mt. xxvi. 6	Mk. xiv. 3	Jn. xii. 2
Τοῦ δὲ Ἰησοῦ γενομένου ἐν Βηθανίᾳ	καὶ ὄντος αὐτοῦ ἐν Βηθανίᾳ	ἐποίησαν οὖν αὐτῷ δεῖπνον ἐκεῖ, καὶ ἡ Μάρθα διηκόνει,
ἐν οἰκίᾳ Σίμωνος τοῦ λεπροῦ,	ἐν τῇ οἰκίᾳ Σίμωνος τοῦ λεπροῦ κατακειμένου αὐτοῦ	ὁ δὲ Λάζαρος εἷς ἦν ἐκ τῶν ἀνακειμένων σὺν αὐτῷ.
προσῆλθεν αὐτῷ γυνὴ ἔχουσα ἀλάβαστρον μύρου	ἦλθεν γυνὴ ἔχουσα ἀλάβαστρον μύρου	ἡ οὖν Μαριὰμ λαβοῦσα λίτραν μύρου
βαρυτίμου	νάρδου πιστικῆς πολυτελοῦς· συντρίψασα τὴν ἀλάβαστρον	νάρδου πιστικῆς πολυτίμου
καὶ κατέχεεν ἐπὶ τῆς κεφαλῆς αὐτοῦ ἀνακειμένου.	κατέχεεν αὐτοῦ τῆς κεφαλῆς.	ἤλειψεν τοὺς πόδας τοῦ Ἰησοῦ καὶ ἐξέμαξεν ταῖς θριξὶν αὐτῆς τοὺς πόδας αὐτοῦ ἡ δὲ οἰκία ἐπληρώθη ἐκ τῆς ὀσμῆς τοῦ μύρου.
ἰδόντες δὲ οἱ μαθηταὶ ἠγανάκτησαν λέγοντες	ἦσαν δέ τινες ἀγανακτοῦντες πρὸς ἑαυτούς	λέγει δὲ Ἰούδας ὁ Ἰσκαριώτης εἷς τῶν μαθητῶν αὐτοῦ, ὁ μέλλων αὐτὸν παραδιδόναι
Εἰς τί ἡ ἀπώλεια αὕτη;	Εἰς τί ἡ ἀπώλεια αὕτη τοῦ μύρου γέγονεν;	Διὰ τί τοῦτο τὸ μύρον οὐκ ἐπράθη
ἐδύνατο γὰρ τοῦτο πραθῆναι πολλοῦ	ἠδύνατο γὰρ τοῦτο τὸ μύρον πραθῆναι ἐπάνω δηναρίων τριακοσίων	τριακοσίων δηναρίων καὶ ἐδόθη πτωχοῖς;
καὶ δοθῆναι πτωχοῖς.	καὶ δοθῆναι τοῖς πτωχοῖς· καὶ ἐνεβριμῶντο αὐτῇ.	κ. τ. λ.
γνοὺς δὲ ὁ Ἰησοῦς εἶπεν αὐτοῖς	ὁ δὲ Ἰησοῦς εἶπεν	εἶπεν οὖν ὁ Ἰησοῦς
Τί κόπους παρέχετε τῇ γυναικί; ἔργον γὰρ καλὸν ἠργάσατο εἰς ἐμέ·	Ἄφετε αὐτήν· τί αὐτῇ κόπους παρέχετε;	Ἄφες αὐτήν,
		ἵνα εἰς τὴν ἡμέραν τοῦ ἐνταφιασμοῦ μου τηρήσῃ αὐτό·
πάντοτε γὰρ τοὺς πτωχοὺς ἔχετε μεθ᾽ ἑαυτῶν,	πάντοτε γὰρ τοὺς πτωχοὺς ἔχετε μεθ᾽ ἑαυτῶν, καὶ ὅταν θέλητε δύνασθε αὐτοῖς πάντοτε εὖ ποιῆσαι,	τοὺς πτωχοὺς γὰρ πάντοτε ἔχετε μεθ᾽ ἑαυτῶν,
ἐμὲ δὲ οὐ πάντοτε ἔχετε·	ἐμὲ δὲ οὐ πάντοτε ἔχετε·	ἐμὲ δὲ οὐ πάντοτε ἔχετε.
βαλοῦσα γὰρ αὕτη τὸ μύρον τοῦτο ἐπὶ τοῦ σώματός μου	ὃ ἔσχεν ἐποίησεν, προέλαβεν μυρίσαι τὸ σῶμά μου	
πρὸς τὸ ἐνταφιάσαι με ἐποίησεν.	εἰς τὸν ἐνταφιασμόν.	

who believe that he must be paraphrasing Mark, are not
really obscure. 'Let her alone in órder that she may keep
it unto the day of my entombment'; that is, 'Do not
interfere with Mary; she has some ointment left, and she
will use the rest at my burial'. This can only mean that
the Fourth Evangelist, or his source, has identified this
woman not only with Mary the sister of Martha, but also
with Mary Magdalene, who, tradition said, had en-
deavoured to anoint the body after the crucifixion. It is
true that St John does not mention the visit of the women
to the tomb for that purpose, and he inserts an account
of the embalming by Joseph which would make the service
of the women superfluous; but old traditions die hard;
he must certainly have heard that the women came to the
sepulchre to anoint the body, and he omits the story
because he prefers the later tradition that Joseph himself
had done all that was necessary. It is significant that he
mentions only Mary in chapter xx.

This incident is of such importance for our enquiry
that it is worth while to compare the Greek text of
Matthew, Mark, and John.

It must be insisted that the list of divergences from the
synoptic accounts is at least as impressive as the former
list, and yet critics simply ignore it.[1] Are we to suppose
that if the Fourth Evangelist had read in 'his copy of
Mark' that a woman poured ointment over the head of
Jesus he would have altered this account into a description

---

[1] Streeter could write: 'An enhanced definiteness and vividness is
given to incidents, recorded separately in Mark or Luke, by bringing
them into connection with one another' (*op. cit.* p. 405). A strange
comment on the confusion of distinct traditions!

of Mary's anointing His feet? The actual genesis of the Johannine account is not hard to determine. There had been current in the Church certain stories: one described a visit to the house of two women, Martha and Mary, one of whom showed her devotion to His Person while the other 'served'; another story related the anointing of Jesus' feet while He sat at meat in the house of Simon; another story, or another version of the same story, described an act of devotion at a meal in Bethany, an act which called forth protests at the apparent waste of precious ointment. There are enough common elements in these stories to make certain some amount of assimilation in the course of oral transmission; all record an act of devotion by a woman, all include a meal, all mention the protests or criticisms of the witnesses. Anyone who has read schoolboys' scripture papers will realize how quickly and inevitably stories run together in just such a way as they appear to have coalesced in the Fourth Gospel. John has taken the general account of the meal from the story of Simon the Leper, but he has introduced elements which belong to the picture of Martha and Mary and to the account of the meal in the house of Simon the Pharisee. Further, he has identified four different women with one another, the nameless woman of Mark, the sinful woman in Galilee, Mary the sister of Martha, and Mary of Magdala. The evangelist was not a schoolboy but a skilled writer, and the improbability of his having done this if the Gospels of Mark and Luke were familiar to him can hardly be exaggerated. On the other hand, it is just the kind of thing likely to occur in a community still dependent on oral tradition.

What then is to be said of his verbal correspondences? Only three are of any real importance; μύρου νάρδου πιστικῆς, τριακοσίων δηναρίων, and τοὺς πτωχοὺς γὰρ πάντοτε ἔχετε μεθ' ἑαυτῶν ἐμὲ δὲ οὐ πάντοτε ἔχετε. All these three are of a kind very easily remembered, striking in character, and therefore likely to become stereotyped in oral tradition. It is true that Matthew, who certainly had Mark before him, did not include the first two; but Matthew is accustomed to prune away Mark's graphic touches, and his omission does not prove that they were not commonly included when the story was told. If it be granted that the incident of the meal at Bethany may often have been related in the churches before Mark included it in his account of the ministry, then there is no reason why the Fourth Evangelist should not have heard it very much as he relates it and with the 'Marcan' phrases. Verbal correspondences are only demonstrative of literary connexion if they cannot be explained in any other way; here they are very easily explained by reference to oral tradition, and they are quite insufficient to destroy the impression of independence created by John's many original features.

To return to the raising of Lazarus; that the whole story grew out of the concluding words of the parable of the rich man and Lazarus, 'if they hear not Moses and the prophets neither will they be persuaded if one rise from the dead', is something more than a mere guess; but there is no need therefore to suppose that our evangelist had read Lk. xvi, or even that he knew the parable. Although he uses the story to illustrate his theme that Jesus is the Resurrection and the Life, there is every indication that he believes himself to be relating history. Yet even a first-century writer would have been puzzled to fit this incident into the Marcan account. St John is not without a sense of history, and the raising of Lazarus fits well into his own scheme; but it is not the scheme of Mark or Luke, and he must have seen the difficulty. Once more it must be repeated that the *onus probandi* lies heavily upon those who maintain that he knew their Gospels.

John xii. 12–19

The Johannine account of the Triumphal Entry provides another passage where a detailed comparison with the Synoptic Gospels is possible. All the Synoptists describe the incident at some length. They are agreed in putting it immediately after Jesus has passed through Jericho, at the end of the long march from the Jordan valley to Jerusalem. John, on the other hand, puts it after the anointing by Mary at Bethany. According to the order of the Fourth Gospel Jesus retired to Ephraim after the raising of Lazarus, and returned to Bethany six days before the Passover. There they made Him a supper, and a great crowd from Jerusalem[1] came out both to see Jesus and also to see Lazarus whom He had raised from the dead. As a result many 'believed'. On the morrow the crowd,[2] since they had heard that Jesus was coming to Jerusalem, took palm branches and went out to meet Him. We may note that whereas in the Synoptists the anointing at Bethany took place several days later, in St John it

[1] ὁ ὄχλος πολὺς ἐκ τῶν 'Ιουδαίων—the great mass of the Jews, not the rulers.

[2] It is specifically stated that they were pilgrims, but probably the same crowd is to be understood.

immediately preceded the triumphal entry. The Fourth
Evangelist is explicit in his statement that the crowd had
come out *from Jerusalem*, though many of them were
pilgrims resident only temporarily in the Holy City. But
in the Synoptists the outburst is spontaneous among the
Galileans who had accompanied Jesus from Jericho. No
reason for their enthusiasm is given except by Matthew,
who in xxi. 10 says, 'And when he was come into
Jerusalem all the city was moved, saying, Who is this?
And the multitudes said, This is the Prophet Jesus from
Nazareth of Galilee'. John explains the popular excite-
ment by reference to the raising of Lazarus. Again,
whereas, according to the Synoptists, the outburst of enthusiasm only began when the multitudes saw Jesus seated
upon the ass, in the Johannine account the demonstration
preceded the finding of the ass, which is added in order
to secure the fulfilment of Zech. ix. 9. Matthew also
quotes this text. The influence of the Old Testament is
perhaps to be traced also in the mention of palm branches
(1 Macc. xiii. 51); Mark says nothing of them, and few
palms grow in Jerusalem.

It would be difficult to pack more contrasts into a short
passage. Yet against this evidence critics who believe
that John knew Mark's Gospel quote the words of acclama-
tion, 'Hosannah! Blessed is he that cometh in the name
of the Lord', which is Mark's wording exactly. John's
addition, 'The King of Israel' is reminiscent of Luke's
'Blessed is he that cometh, even the King, in the name
of the Lord'. Once more it must be noted that the
common element is a brief saying such as would be easily
remembered. The picture as a whole is entirely different,

and the most probable conclusion is that John was following an independent tradition.

John xii. 20–50

It is doubtful whether the rest of chapter xii, which describes the visit of the Greeks and the discourse of Jesus which follows, has any direct bearing on our enquiry. Perhaps the evangelist corrects some ideas which underly the synoptic narratives (e.g. that Jesus prayed that the cup might pass from Him, or that an angel would presume to speak to Him), but there is certainly no evidence here of literary dependence.

One verse of chapter xii is worthy of special notice. St John has few sayings of Jesus which are also recorded by the Synoptists, but in xii. 25 he has the famous pronouncement concerning the losing and saving of life. His version may be set beside that of Mark:

Jn. xii. 25	Mk. viii. 35
ὁ φιλῶν. τὴν ψυχὴν αὐτοῦ ἀπολλύει αὐτήν, καὶ ὁ μισῶν τὴν ψυχὴν αὐτοῦ ἐν τῷ κόσμῳ τούτῳ εἰς ζωὴν αἰώνιον φυλάξει αὐτήν.	ὃς γὰρ ἐὰν θέλῃ τὴν ἑαυτοῦ ψυχὴν σῶσαι ἀπολέσει αὐτήν. ὃς δ' ἂν ἀπολέσει τὴν ψυχὴν αὐτοῦ ἕνεκεν ἐμοῦ καὶ τοῦ εὐαγγελίου σώσει αὐτήν.

Could divergence be wider?

John xiii

The main divergences of St John from the synoptic accounts of the Last Supper are too well known to require emphasis here. He contradicts the Marcan dating of the supper, and he omits all mention of the institution of the Eucharist, substituting his account of the washing of the

disciples' feet. In these respects he must have been deliberately modifying a widely-accepted tradition, whether
he knew that tradition in written documents or not; and
he must have had strong reasons for so doing. What were
those reasons it is not our present task to enquire. We can
only say that he gives no evidence that he is conscious of
correcting a written Gospel, and the whole chapter is
remarkably lacking in verbal correspondences. The following points have been noted:

1. Jn. xiii. 2: 'And during supper the devil having
already put into the heart of Judas Iscariot, Simon's son,
to betray him' etc.

Luke xxii. 3: 'And Satan entered into Judas who was
called Iscariot, being of the number of the twelve. And
he went away' etc.

Only Luke and John refer to the devil as responsible
for the betrayal, but there are no verbal similarities, and
the idea would easily suggest itself to Christian thought.
There is nothing in the Synoptists to correspond with
John's account of the question of the Beloved Disciple,
or of the giving of the sop.

2. Jn. xiii. 16: 'Verily, verily, I say unto you, A servant
is not greater than his lord, nor one sent (ἀπόστολος)
greater than he that sent him.'

Mt. x. 24: 'A disciple is not above his master, nor a
servant above his lord' (cp. Lk. vi. 40). Literary dependence will hardly be alleged; it is clear that the saying in
some form was well remembered in the Church.

3. Jn. xiii. 21: 'Verily, verily, I say unto you, that one
of you will betray me.'

Mk. xiv. 18: 'Verily I say unto you, that one of you will

betray me.' Here the correspondence is exact; but again, this is a short and striking saying such as would be most easily remembered. 'Such solemn words would be likely to be remembered in one and the same form' (Plummer). The dismay of the disciples when they hear the words is quite differently described.

In this chapter the case for the dependence of John rests rather upon the order of events than upon the few verbal similarities. We may conveniently compare Mark and John:

Mark	John
The making of the supper.	The making of the supper.
The prediction of betrayal.	The devil entering into Judas.
The conversation following.	
The eucharist.	The foot washing.
The prediction of Peter's denial.	The prediction of betrayal.
Peter's declaration.	Conversation following.
	Discourse on the coming glorification and departure of Jesus.
	Peter's declaration, leading to Prediction of Peter's denial.

Correspondence is by no means exact, but broadly speaking the order is the same, if we omit the foot-washing from John and the eucharist from Mark. But the fact supplies little reason for concluding that John's account is founded on that of Mark. We have every reason to believe that the passion narrative took definite shape at an early period in the history of the Church, and therefore any evangelist who produced a written account would be likely to follow roughly the accepted order. He might omit or add as he pleased, but his general outline would be in accordance with accepted tradition.[1]

John xvi. 32

We may pass over the discourses which follow, but there is one verse which is worthy of note. 'Do ye now believe? Behold the hour cometh and is come that ye will be scattered every one of you, and will leave me alone.' Here at any rate the Fourth Gospel shows no knowledge of Luke, nor indeed is the verse consistent with his own picture of the disciples gathering in Jerusalem on the first day of the week and receiving at once an assurance of the resurrection. Macgregor remarks that the words are an echo of Mk. xiv. 27, Mt. xxvi. 31, 'All ye will be offended, because it is written, I will smite the shepherd, and the sheep will be scattered'. We may rather say that both passages echo an early tradition that after the crucifixion the disciples fled, and as soon as it was considered safe they returned to Galilee to their own homes.[2] This is one of a few very interesting passages in which the Fourth Gospel witnesses to the survival of a pre-synoptic tradition. We miss the point if we think of the author as merely revising the Synoptic Gospels.

[1] Goguel notes that Lk. xxii. 34 and Jn. xiii. 38 both put the prediction of Peter's denial *after supper*, and he sees a correspondence between Lk. xxii. 24–30 with its exhortation to service, and the foot-washing in Jn. xiii. 4–13. But these resemblances are rather distant, and can hardly be pressed to imply literary dependence in the face of the much wider and more striking dissimilarities between the two accounts.

[2] Cp. *The Gospel of Peter* vii: 'And I with my fellows was in sorrow, and being wounded at heart we hid ourselves, for we were sought for by them as malefactors, and as minded to burn the Temple.' This can only be a fragment of early tradition, for it would not have been invented in the second century.

Chapter V

JOHN XVIII AND XIX

WE NOW proceed to the study of St John's account of the trial and crucifixion of Jesus, and here if anywhere we should suppose that if he was familiar with the Synoptic Gospels the fact would be unmistakably apparent. But we must proceed cautiously, for here it is more than ever necessary to beware of the assumption that if the Fourth Evangelist introduces features which appear in one or other of the synoptic writers he is necessarily dependent for his knowledge upon the earlier Gospel. As we have said, the passion narrative took shape at a very early period, probably long before Mark wrote his Gospel, and every Christian of the second or third generation, indeed every Christian of the first generation, must have been to some extent familiar with its outline, whether he read it in a written document or not.

John xviii. 1–11

The Fourth Gospel agrees with the others that Jesus went straight from the supper across the Kedron, although he does not speak of the Mount of Olives nor call the garden 'Gethsemane'. Luke says that 'Jesus went according to his custom to the Mount of Olives' (xxii. 39), and John says that 'Judas knew the place, for Jesus often resorted thither with his disciples' (xviii. 2). It is claimed that here we have a clear indication of the influence of Luke upon John. It is a stronger point than many of those

commonly advanced, and if there were many such accidental correspondences the case for the dependence of
John would be deserving of more respect than we are
inclined to pay to it. But by itself it is by no means conclusive. Both evangelists may reproduce a genuine historical reminiscence, and if it is objected that the Fourth
Evangelist was not much concerned with historical details
as such, the answer is that here he may have been anxious
to meet the kind of charge made later by Celsus, that
Jesus hid to escape arrest. He tells us therefore that Judas
would have no difficulty in finding Jesus because the
garden across the Kedron had been a favourite meeting-
place of the disciples in the last week; and that may very
well be true. Perhaps the disciples were staying at
Bethany (Mk. xi. 11), or perhaps they bivouacked on the
slopes of Olivet, as Luke seems to imply (xxi. 37). In
either case the Garden of Gethsemane may have been a
rendezvous for Jesus and His immediate followers, and if
so, it is not really surprising that Luke and John should
both state that Jesus had been accustomed to resort
thither.

Certainly John's account of the coming of Judas bears
little resemblance to that of Luke. We need not emphasize
his omission of the agony and the kiss of Judas; dogmatic
interests would provide a sufficient explanation here; but
why, if he had Mark or Luke in mind, did he say that the
Roman garrison was concerned in the arrest? It was not
the wish of any of the evangelists to represent the Romans
as concerned in the affair of Jesus until appeal was made
to Pilate by the Sanhedrin, and they are agreed that no
considerable resistance was made. This is another passage

in which St John may preserve a trace of a primitive tradition. It is by no means inconceivable that there may have been negotiations between the Jews and the Romans before the arrest of Jesus, and the Romans may have sent soldiers to support the high-priestly party in case of serious resistance. If so, it must be supposed that the disappearance of the Romans from the synoptic account is due to the conviction that the Jews were solely responsible for the arrest of Jesus, and John here takes us back behind the earliest synoptic account. The alternative explanation, that John adds a mention of the cohort 'for dramatic and symbolical reasons', is not altogether satisfying, for he, even more than the other evangelists, is concerned to fasten the guilt upon the Jews. Nor is it certain that the Romans, if they had been present, would have taken Jesus to Pilate at once, and not allowed the High-Priest to try the case. Pilate may have been anxious not to intervene more than was necessary, as indeed appears from the record of the subsequent trial. His business was to keep order, no easy task at the Passover; and by sending a detachment of soldiers to reinforce the Temple police he may have displayed no more than ordinary caution.

For the rest, the Johannine account is no doubt the author's own composition intended to express the complete independence of Jesus, and to excuse the desertion of the disciples. There is no need to assume familiarity with Mark because John knew the tradition that at this point the disciples forsook Jesus and fled.

The dramatic incident of the attack upon the servant of the High-Priest is described by all the evangelists, and the Johannine account displays both agreement and disagreement with the others.

John only says that it was Simon Peter who drew his sword, an improbable identification in view of the silence of the Synoptists. He only tells us that the servant's name was Malchus. The words καὶ ἔπαισεν τὸν τοῦ ἀρχιερέως δοῦλον are almost exactly those of Mark, whereas Matthew has πατάξας and Luke ἐπάταξεν. John also uses the word ὠτάριον, otherwise peculiar to Mark; he adds, however, as does Luke, that it was the *right* ear that Peter cut off. John's βάλε τὴν μάχαιραν εἰς τὴν θήκην is in no way reminiscent of Matthew's Ἀπόστρεψον τὴν μάχαιράν σου εἰς τὸν τόπον αὐτῆς, and the question 'the cup which my Father hath given me, shall I not drink it?' though perhaps intended to correct the synoptic tradition that Jesus had prayed 'Let this cup pass from me', does not imply more than a general acquaintance with the tradition embodied in the Synoptic Gospels. This is a short account of a dramatic incident where we should expect considerable uniformity in the traditions. Any writer who described how a follower of Jesus drew his sword and cut off the ear of one of the servants of the High-Priest could hardly avoid using some words that appear in other accounts, particularly if he was writing at a time when oral tradition concerning famous incidents had become to some extent stereotyped. Yet of St John's forty-nine Greek words about thirty are peculiar to his own account, and he uses εἵλκυσεν, ἀπέκοψεν, βάλε, and θήκην for Mark's σπασάμενος, ἀφεῖλεν, and Matthew's ἀπόστρεψον and τόπον.

John xviii. 13–24

The Fourth Evangelist says that the cohort and the chiliarch and the servants of the Jews took Jesus bound to Annas first. It has been suggested that in this verse the author betrays knowledge of Luke, who in iii. 2 says that John the Baptist began his ministry in the high-priesthood of Annas and Caiaphas. This suggestion need not detain us. We do not know the source of St John's belief that Jesus was taken to Annas first, or what was the exact position of Annas at this time,[1] but it is not impossible that he took some part in the preliminary enquiry. If we accept the very probable guess that there is some dislocation in the text here, and that verse 24 should follow verse 13, then the trial which follows takes place before Caiaphas, not before Annas. In any case the Johannine account owes nothing to Mk. xiv. 55–64. The High-Priest interrogates Jesus 'concerning his disciples and concerning his teaching', but no charge is brought, and there is no mention of the threat to the Temple or of the claim to be the Messiah. The reply of Jesus is not suggestive of anything contained in the Synoptic Gospels, 'Why askest thou me? Ask those who have heard what I said to them'. No witnesses are called, as in Matthew and Mark. Without delay they hurry Jesus away to the Praetorium.

John xviii. 15–18, 25–27

All the evangelists narrate the threefold denial of Peter, and we may well believe that no story was better known

---

[1] He had been deposed from the high-priesthood in A.D. 15 by Valerius Gratus, but the office remained in his family.

in the early Church. But the divergences between the several accounts are remarkable, particularly between Mk. xiv. 66–72 and Lk. xxii. 56–62. John's narrative seems independent of both. He says that Simon Peter and another disciple followed to the High-Priest's house. The other disciple was known to the High-Priest, and was therefore allowed to enter; but Peter stood without, until the other disciple spoke to the door-keeper and brought him in. It was then that the maid who kept the door challenged Peter, 'Art thou not also one of this man's disciples?' The curt reply, 'I am not', is in contrast with the οὐκ οἶδα which appears in all the Synoptists. In the first three Gospels the narrative of Peter's denials is continuous, but as the text stands John interposes the account of the trial before the High-Priest, returning to Peter in verse 25. 'Simon Peter continued standing and warming himself. Therefore *they* said to him, Art thou not also one of his disciples?' Mark ascribes the second challenge to the same maidservant, Matthew has ἄλλη and Luke ἕτερος. John's only agreement with Luke is in Peter's reply, 'I am not'. The third denial in the Fourth Gospel is in answer to 'one of the servants of the High-Priest, a kinsman of him whose ear Peter had cut off'. This man exclaims: 'Did I not see thee in the garden with him?' There is no mention of Peter's Galilean speech, or of his cursing and swearing; nor are we told that Peter went out to weep. The Johannine account reads like history, but it provides no evidence of dependence on the Synoptists. On the theory of dependence some explanation would be required of changes which have no dogmatic significance.

John xviii. 28–40

It is generally admitted that the Johannine account of
the trial before Pilate seems at first sight to be quite
independent of the Synoptists. Jesus is taken to the
Praetorium, into which the Jews refuse to enter for fear
of ceremonial defilement. Pilate therefore goes out to
them and asks what charge they bring. They answer
vaguely, 'If this man were not a malefactor, we would not
have delivered him unto thee'. Pilate suggests that the
Jews should deal with the case themselves, to which they
reply that it is not lawful for them to put any man to
death. We are not concerned with the historicity of this
account, we need only point out that not a word of it
appears to be derived from the Synoptists.

The following verses are at least reminiscent of Mk.
xv. 2 ff. 'Therefore Pilate entered again into the Praetorium
and called Jesus and said to him Σὺ εἶ ὁ βασιλεὺς τῶν
'Ιουδαίων'—the exact words recorded in Mk. xv. 2. But
the answer of Jesus is unexpected: 'Dost thou say this of
thyself, or did others tell it thee concerning me?' Pilate
replies, 'Am I a Jew? Thy nation and the chief priests
delivered thee unto me. What hast thou done?' The
contrast with the synoptic account at least suggests that,
despite the one sentence which is common, Mark is not
John's source here. That Pilate had asked Jesus 'Art thou
the King of the Jews?' would pass rapidly into accepted
tradition. That all the Gospels record the utterance is no
proof that they were mutually dependent.

Very tentatively another suggestion may be put forward.
It is just possible that in the Fourth Gospel Pilate's words

should not be read as a question but as a declaration, 'Thou art the King of the Jews'. Such an interpretation would give point to the reply of Jesus which is otherwise obscure, and would explain Pilate's superscription on the cross, 'Jesus of Nazareth the King of the Jews', a title to which the Jews took great exception (xix. 19–22). The statement that the title was written in Hebrew and Greek and Latin for the whole world to read has long been recognized as significant, but its true force is only seen when it is realized that the Fourth Evangelist wishes to represent Pilate as proclaiming to the world his own acceptance of the claims of Jesus in contrast with the Jews who deliver Him up to be crucified. St John seizes the opportunity of explaining that the kingdom of Jesus is not of this world, to which Pilate replies Οὐκοῦν βασιλεὺς εἶ σύ—So you are a king![1] To which Jesus answers by emphasizing his original confession ' *Thou* sayest that I am a King'.[2] Critics have been so long accustomed to read St John with the assumption in mind that he knew St Mark, that they have taken his words here in the Marcan sense and missed their real significance.

It is sometimes argued that since we are not told by the Fourth Evangelist that the Jews had made any definite charge against Jesus a knowledge of the synoptic narrative must be assumed, otherwise Pilate could not have gone straight to the point of the kingship. But this is to attribute to the Fourth Evangelist a purely historical realism which is not in keeping with his manifest intentions. He wishes

[1] οὐκοῦν with no negative force—*therefore, then, accordingly* (Liddell and Scott). There is no need to take the sentence as interrogative.

[2] Perhaps a reminiscence of the synoptic tradition Σὺ λέγεις, but proving no literary connexion.

to present Pilate as confessing the kingship of Jesus; that for him is the true significance of the trial, and any previous witness of the Jews is expressly repudiated. In verse 38 Pilate goes out to the Jews and makes his declaration, Ἐγὼ οὐδεμίαν εὑρίσκω ἐν αὐτῷ αἰτίαν. This is near to Lk. xxiii. 4: Οὐδὲν εὑρίσκω αἴτιον ἐν τῷ ἀνθρώπῳ τούτῳ, but the emphasis on the pronoun in John must be noted. The setting is quite different, and a short confession such as this might well be drawn from oral sources. The same may be said of Pilate's question, βούλεσθε οὖν ἀπολύσω ὑμῖν τὸν βασιλέα τῶν Ἰουδαίων; Mark has θέλετε ἀπολύσω ὑμῖν τὸν βασιλέα τῶν Ἰουδαίων; but he makes it Pilate's answer to the crowd's demand that he should do as he was wont, and there is nothing in Mark to correspond to the Johannine statement that it was Pilate who reminded them of the Pascal custom. It is difficult to see why the Fourth Evangelist should have gone out of his way to rewrite Mark in these small particulars; but it is not difficult to think of him as knowing from oral sources that the Governor had said, 'Do you wish me to release the King of the Jews?'

The argument that here again the evangelist must have had the Synoptists in mind because he introduces Barabbas without previously explaining who he was is particularly weak. No doubt every Christian had heard of Barabbas, and it was for Christians that John wrote. Besides, his account gains greatly in dramatic force by the post-ponement of the climax, 'And Barabbas was a robber'. The other Gospels describe him as guilty of insurrection and murder, which is hardly the same thing, and it is arbitrary to suppose that John deliberately changes the description 'the better to use him as a foil to the rejected king' (Macgregor).

John xix. 1–16

The chapter opens with the mention of the scourging, an obscure feature in the synoptic accounts. According to Mark, followed by Matthew, the scourging took place after sentence of crucifixion had been passed, and it would seem to be no more than a piece of wanton cruelty. Lk. xxiii. 16 mentions it only as a suggestion of Pilate's, alternative to the death sentence, 'I will therefore chastise him and let him go'. But in John the scourging falls into place as part of the examination of the prisoner, exactly what a Roman magistrate generally did in the effort to extract evidence. The comparison with Acts xxii. 24 is obvious. Once more we note that the Fourth Evangelist, untrammeled by knowledge of the Marcan story, is able to give a better historical account, even though 'history' was not the main purpose of his work.

That it was at this point that the soldiers gave play to their sense of humour, as John says, is no more improbable than the statement that the mocking followed the final condemnation. In other particulars there is nothing to prove that the evangelist was influenced by the Marcan account. He has the cry 'Hail, King of the Jews', and he mentions the purple robe and the blows (Mk. xv. 19), but we need look no further than the universal tradition of the Church as a source for such details. If it were a written Gospel on which John drew why did he turn Mark's καὶ ἔτυπτον αὐτοῦ τὴν κεφαλὴν καλάμῳ into the weaker καὶ ἐδίδοσαν αὐτῷ ῥαπίσματα?

Once more Pilate goes out to the people (verse 4), and again he testifies that he finds no fault in Jesus. Jesus stands before them, the true King, with His royal robe of purple and His crown of thorns. Pilate presents Him to the Jews, 'Behold the man!' Then at last the chief priests disclose their infamy by demanding death by crucifixion, and Pilate replies, 'Take ye him and crucify him, for I find no fault in him!' Indeed, a bold rewriting of Mark! It may be objected that Pilate can never have said this, for the Jews had no right to crucify, but in dramatic power the scene far exceeds anything in the Synoptic Gospels.

Pilate's repeated suggestion that the Jews should deal with the case themselves leads the chief priests to reveal the real cause of their animosity. Momentarily off their guard, they cry, 'We have a law, and by the law he ought to die, because he made himself Son of God'. Pilate hearing this is the more afraid, and he examines Jesus once more. 'Whence art thou?' When Jesus gives no answer Pilate reminds Him of his authority, 'Speakest thou not to me?' Here no doubt we are reminded of Mk. xv. 5: 'But Jesus no longer answered anything, so that Pilate marvelled', and of Lk. xxiii. 9: 'And Herod questioned him in many words, but he answered him nothing.' These two synoptic passages prove that there was a firmly established belief that Jesus at His trial had refused to answer questions, but some said that the refusal was to Pilate and some to Herod. There is no need to conclude that because John worked the tradition into his narrative he had read either Mark or Luke.

Pilate's final attempt to release Jesus is defeated by the Jews who bring forward their last argument, 'If thou let this man go, thou art not Caesar's friend; for everyone

that maketh himself a king speaketh against Caesar'. No
more is heard of the religious charge, which had had the
wrong effect, but the Jews press home the political point.
Pilate dares not resist, but before delivering Jesus to the
Jews he performs one last service. He enthrones Jesus on
the tribunal,[1] and presents Him to His subjects, 'Behold
your King!' It has been said that the Governor is making
one last attempt to have the case laughed out of court;
more probably the evangelist is pursuing his theme that
Pilate acknowledged the Kingship of Jesus. The exact
place and time are stated, 'It was the day of Preparation,
about the sixth hour'. This is the climax of the drama.
'They cried out therefore, Away with him, away with
him, crucify him. Pilate saith to them, Shall I crucify
your king? The chief priests answered, We have no king
but Caesar. Then therefore he delivered him *to them* that
he might be crucified.' The iniquity of the Jews was
fulfilled.

Again, we are not concerned with the historicity of the
Johannine narrative, but with the question whether or
not it is founded on a knowledge of the Synoptists. It is
difficult to imagine an account further removed from
theirs.[2] St Mark's Gospel is contradicted in the statement
that it was the Preparation for the Passover, and in the
note of time, 'about noon'. The Fourth Evangelist may
have had some symbolic interest in mind here, though
what it may have been is not obvious. But more probably
he had other, and perhaps better, sources of information.

---

[1] ἐκάθισεν ἐπὶ βήματος is unquestionably transitive. *The Gospel of Peter* (§III) has a similar tradition.

[2] 'The fact chiefly deserving of notice is perhaps that the Fourth Evangelist who (as it seems) knew St Mark has treated him with so much independence' (Stanton, *op. cit.* p. 262).

Is there any positive indication that he was influenced by our written Gospels? Only those who forget that all traditions were not written traditions will answer this question with any confidence in the affirmative. St John's is an entirely independent account.

John xix. 17–24

One of the most striking features of the Johannine account of the crucifixion is the statement that Jesus carried His cross for Himself. This is probably intended as a direct contradiction of the tradition embodied in the Synoptists that Simon of Cyrene was pressed into the service. Perhaps the suggestion had already been made that Simon was crucified instead of Jesus, although we only hear of it at a much later date.[1] It is not impossible, of course, that Jesus began by carrying the cross and was subsequently relieved of it, for if Simon was coming in from the country (Mk. xv. 21) they would probably meet him somewhere near the city gate; but John's βαστάζων αὐτῷ τὸν σταυρόν seems emphatic, and if he did not know the Docetic theory we must suppose that he had the parallel with Isaac in mind (Gen. xxii. 6).

The evangelist represents the Jews as still chiefly concerned, 'Pilate delivered him to them to be crucified, and they took Jesus'; but he allows that the actual crucifixion was the work of the soldiers. For the rest, John's description follows the synoptic tradition fairly closely. He mentions the robbers, though he merely calls them ἄλλους δύο, and he says nothing more about them until verse 32, when he states that their legs were broken —an independent feature. He then describes at length

[1] Irenaeus, I. 24. 4.

Pilate's action in writing a title (τίτλον, cp. the synoptic ἐπιγραφήν), '*Jesus of Nazareth*, the King of the Jews'. He alone mentions the protest of the chief priests and Pilate's curt rejoinder. *After* describing this little controversy he tells of the parting of the garments, quoting Ps. xxii. 18, but with verbal differences as compared with Mk. xv. 24, and with an expanded account of the soldiers' conduct, which may be due to a desire to make the fulfilment of prophecy more complete, but which has no parallel in the Synoptists. Despite essential similarities, we may say that St John's narrative is independent. The evangelist reproduces the main features of the common tradition, but in his own order and in his own way.

John xix. 25–27

It is generally admitted that these verses cannot be reconciled with any of the synoptic accounts. This is not the place to discuss the origin or significance of the tradition, but it is clear that if the evangelist thought of the cross as surrounded by a group of women and the Beloved Disciple he cannot have had the synoptic accounts in mind. All the other Gospels state that the women stood watching from afar, and of course they know nothing of the Beloved Disciple. It is noteworthy that the names of the women are not those given by Mark:

Mk. xv. 40	Jn. xix. 25
And there were women beholding from afar, amongst whom were Mary Magdalene, and Mary the mother of James the Less and Joses, and Salome... and many others.	Now there were standing by the cross of Jesus his Mother, and his Mother's sister, Mary the wife of Clopas, and Mary Magdalene.

Without forced identifications, there is only one name in common, and the Synoptists all omit the Virgin! Surely it must be admitted that the Fourth Evangelist has drawn on another stream of tradition.

John xix. 28–37

The death of Jesus is described briefly and with dignity. The evangelist says nothing about the darkness at midday, and indeed he is thinking of a later hour (xix. 14); he omits the cry of despair, the rending of the veil, and the Lucan account of the penitent robber; he ignores alike the blasphemous revilings of the spectators and the testimony of the centurion. St John is mainly interested in the completion of the fulfilment of prophecy, and he tells us ἵνα τελειωθῇ ἡ γραφὴ λέγει, Διψῶ. The offering of the vinegar may be compared with the action of 'a certain man' in Mark, but there is little verbal correspondence:

Mk. xv. 36	Jn. xix. 29
δραμὼν δέ τις γεμίσας σπόγγον ὄξους περιθεὶς καλάμῳ ἐπότιζεν αὐτόν.	σκεῦος ἔκειτο ὄξους μεστόν· σπόγγον οὖν μεστὸν τοῦ ὄξους ὑσσώπῳ περιθέντες προσήνεγκαν αὐτοῦ τῷ στόματι.

It is the same tradition, and that is as much as we can say.

Mark says that in the evening, since it was the Preparation, Joseph of Arimathea went boldly to Pilate and asked for the body of Jesus. John introduces the same consideration, but in quite a different way. The Jews were concerned lest the bodies should remain upon the crosses on the Sabbath, so they asked Pilate that their legs might be broken, and the bodies removed. The legs of the robbers were broken, but since Jesus was found to be dead already a soldier pierced His side. Thus the Scripture was fulfilled, 'A bone of him shall not be broken', and 'They shall look on him whom they pierced'. We do not know the source from which St John derived this tradition, or why he attached to it so much importance. He did not derive it from the Synoptic Gospels which contain no hint of anything of the kind. The claim that the narrative rests upon the testimony of an eye-witness is one of the puzzles of the Fourth Gospel.

John xix. 38–42

Almost equally remote from the synoptic account is the Johannine description of the burial. Joseph of Arimathea, 'being a disciple, but secretly for fear of the Jews', asked[1] Pilate that he might take away the body of Jesus; and Pilate gave him leave. So he removed the body, and he and Nicodemus bound it in linen cloths with a hundred pounds of spices. Then they laid it in a new tomb in a garden near by. There is 'an echo' of Luke here, for Luke says καὶ ἔθηκεν αὐτὸν ἐν μνήματι λαξευτῷ οὗ οὐκ ἦν οὐδεὶς οὔπω κείμενος, and John has καὶ ἐν τῷ κήπῳ μνημεῖον καινόν, ἐν ᾧ οὐδέπω οὐδεὶς ἦν τεθειμένος. But the echo is distant, and we need postulate no other source for John's statement that the tradition soon established (Mt. xxvii. 60) that the tomb was a new one and therefore the sacred body was not defiled by the proximity of any other corpse.[2] Much more significant is the fact that John contradicts the important synoptic tradition that the

---

[1] ἠρώτησεν: all the Synoptists have ἠτήσατο.

[2] Streeter is inclined to accept the reading κενόν for καινόν in Jn. xix. 41, and to account for καινόν as due to assimilation to Matthew (*op. cit.* p. 412).

Lord's body was hastily buried without the usual spices. It is of course possible that John wished to correct the synoptic account, either from motives of reverence, or to put the death of Jesus still further beyond the possibility of doubt; but if he had known and respected the Second and Third Gospels he could hardly have introduced his account of the elaborate embalming by Joseph and Nicodemus.

Chapter VI

JOHN XX AND XXI. THE RESURRECTION

THE DIFFICULTIES of St John's account of the Resurrection are notorious, and the importance of its bearing on our present enquiry hardly needs to be emphasized. The resurrection of Jesus was the most prominent fact of early Christian tradition, and the evidence on which it rested must have been constantly rehearsed from the time of St Peter to the end of the first century and beyond. One might have supposed that in this respect tradition would soon have become stereotyped, and the Church would soon have had a clear and consistent account to present to the world; and yet nowhere is it more difficult to harmonize the Gospel narratives. We can only suppose that from the very first there were ambiguities and uncertainties in the evidence, and that in the attempt to remove those ambiguities and resolve those uncertainties traditions developed in different directions among different groups of Christian believers.

John xx has so little in common with Mark xvi that we might have argued that the fact is in itself enough to prove the independence of the Fourth Gospel, but it must be admitted that Luke's divergence from Mark is hardly less striking, and he at least had the Second Gospel before him. The contrast between Luke and Mark proves that in the latter part of the first century inconsistent traditions concerning the resurrection were current in the Church, and an evangelist must make his choice. We must discard

the old idea of a writer wholly dependent upon the written
work of his predecessors.

John xx. 1, 2

The Fourth Evangelist speaks of one woman only who
came to the sepulchre. It is true that in verse 2 he uses
a plural verb, 'We know not where they have laid him',
and this may be a survival of the earlier tradition that
several women came to the tomb on the morning of the
first day of the week. But it is strange that one who is
thought to have been familiar with two at least of our
Gospels should have departed so remarkably from their
account. Nor is the problem solved by supposing that
since Mary has so small a part to play, and since she was
not allowed to be the chief witness of the resurrection,
there was no need to mention her companions. That may
explain why in the development of the Johannine tradition
the other women dropped out, but it does not help us to
conceive of the Fourth Evangelist as himself deliberately
altering an account familiar in Mark and Luke. In oral
narration the other women, since they had no part to
play, might well be forgotten, but not when their place
had been secured by their inclusion in a written narrative
accepted and read in the churches.

John's tradition, believing that Joseph and Nicodemus
had embalmed the body of Jesus, could not enlarge on
the part of the women, so it was believed that Mary saw
only the stone taken away from the mouth of the sepulchre.
Even here the words used to describe her discovery are
not such as we might expect of an author familiar with
the Synoptic Gospels. 'She seeth the stone taken away

out of the sepulchre' (ἠρμένον ἐκ τοῦ μνημείου). Mark
says that the women saw that it had been rolled back.
Why this change to a less graphic phrase, unless someone
unfamiliar with the nature of a Jewish tomb in the
neighbourhood of Jerusalem had had a hand in the
shaping of tradition? Mary makes no further investigation; it seems almost as though she is hurried off the stage
lest she should learn too much and thus anticipate the
discovery of the empty tomb by the disciples. 'She
runneth and cometh to Simon Peter and to the other
disciple whom Jesus loved, and saith unto them, They
have taken away the Lord out of the sepulchre, and we
know not where they have laid him.' If the evangelist
had Mark in mind, clearly he was determined to dis-
regard him.

John xx. 3–10

The examination of the tomb which Luke ascribes to the
women (Lk. xxiv. 3) is here transferred to Simon Peter
and the Beloved Disciple. That behind this form of the
tradition there lies a desire to make men and not women
the chief witnesses of the resurrection we may well believe.
But even so, there is hardly a word in the Johannine
account reminiscent of the narratives of the other Gospels.
Once more we must ask which is more probable, that the
profound changes here manifest in the earlier account
took place during the period of oral transmission, or
that they are the deliberate work of the evangelist himself?

It is not impossible to trace the process by which
tradition developed. At an early period it was known

that the women who came to the sepulchre had failed to find the body of Jesus, and that they had had a brief interview with a young man who told them that the body of Jesus was not there (Mk. xvi. 5, 6). From that simple tradition development had been on divergent lines. In the circle to which Matthew belonged it was believed that the women had seen an angel descend from heaven and roll away the stone. Luke had heard that the women went into the sepulchre and saw two angels who rebuked them for seeking the living among the dead. In other circles before the end of the first century development had gone much further. Somehow the conviction had grown up that the evidence of the empty tomb rested upon the testimony of two of the disciples, and the part of the women was almost forgotten, though one woman was allowed to have been instrumental in bringing the disciples to the sepulchre. This is John's conception of the course of events. There can be no doubt that his version is late as compared with the narrative of Mark, but there is no justification for the conclusion that the Johannine tradition is a development of that embodied in Luke. Dr Streeter wrote, 'The visit of Peter and another disciple to the tomb recorded by John gives precision to the Lucan statement that "Certain of those with us went to the tomb, and found even as the women had said, but him they saw not".'[1] Rather Lk. xxiv. 24 marks the first stage of an attempt to provide better evidence for the empty tomb than that of the women. John embodies this attempt at a later stage, but there is nothing in John to suggest that he had read Luke with whose account he

[1] The *Four Gospels*, p. 406.

is otherwise in almost complete disagreement. One point is worthy of notice. In verse 9 we read that 'as yet they knew not the scripture that he must rise from the dead'. Even in John's tradition it has not been quite forgotten that the disciples were not prepared for the resurrection, although, according to Mark, Jesus had three times prophesied His resurrection in unmistakable terms.

John xx. 11–18

In verse 11 we seem to rejoin the synoptic tradition. Mary Magdalene reappears at the sepulchre, where she stands weeping, and stooping she looks down into the sepulchre. This is at least faintly reminiscent of the synoptic account in which the women stand outside the tomb. According to John, Mary sees two angels sitting in the sepulchre, and they ask her the cause of her grief; to which she replies in the words already addressed to Peter, 'They have taken away my Lord, and I know not where they have laid him'. The story does not hang well together, for the disciples have already been convinced of the resurrection by the evidence of the empty tomb. Presumably we are to suppose that Mary was not in the garden when the disciples made their discovery. But if we omit the appeal of Mary to Peter and the Beloved Disciple we have a fairly consistent narrative which is not unlike that of the Synoptists. The tradition is clearly the same, but the form in which it appears certainly does not suggest literary dependence.

It is often said that because John mentions *two* angels in the sepulchre it may be inferred that he had read Lk.

xxiv. 4. Yet how completely different are the two accounts! In Luke, the women enter and search the tomb; in John, Mary stands without and looks down. In Luke, the angels rebuke the women for their failure to anticipate the resurrection; in John, they have nothing more to say. In Luke, they remind the women of the prophecy of Jesus while He was yet in Galilee, and the women hurry away to proclaim their tidings; in John, the announcement of the resurrection is reserved for Jesus Himself, and the angels have no real place in the narrative. It is very remarkable that so many critics should have been impressed by one common feature in the two accounts, and apparently blind to the fundamental differences between the two narratives. The most that can be said is that at some stage in their development the two streams of tradition had been in contact, but we have no reason to suppose that the Lucan presentation is an intermediate stage between Mark and John.

In other ways the earliest tradition developed along divergent lines. Mark tells us of the interview of the women with a young man. It would not be long before various suggestions were made as to the identity of this young man. The most obvious suggestion was that he was an angel, and that is probably what Mark intends us to understand. In Matthew we are left in no doubt that he was an angel, and in Luke and in *The Gospel of Peter* he has become two angels. But there was another possibility; might not the young man have been Jesus Himself, whom the women for some reason failed to recognize? Or did they recognize Him? Tradition developed also in this direction, and in Matthew we have a clear doublet of the conversation with the angel in the conversation between Jesus and the women in which Jesus repeats the angel's message (Mt. xxviii. 7 and 10).

John is influenced by both traditions in their developed form. He, like Luke, has the two angels, but he also records an appearance of Jesus Himself, of which Luke seems to have been ignorant (xxiv. 24). Thus both Matthew and John have adopted traditions which embody alternative explanations of the identity of the young man.

It is interesting therefore to compare the accounts of Matthew and John. In Mt. xxviii. 9f. we read, 'And behold, Jesus met them saying, All hail. And they came and took hold of his feet, and worshipped him. Then saith Jesus unto them, Fear not; go tell my brethren that they depart into Galilee, and there they shall see me.' According to John, Mary, still standing near the sepulchre, turns and sees Jesus, whom she mistakes for the gardener—an interesting survival of the earlier belief that the women did not know who it was who spoke to them. Jesus repeats the question of the angels, and Mary replies, 'Sir, if thou hast borne him hence, tell me where thou hast laid him, and I will take him away'. Jesus discloses His identity, and tells Mary not to touch Him, for He is not yet ascended to the Father. 'But go to my brethren, and say to them, I ascend to my Father and your Father, to my God and your God.' Mary Magdalene returns to the disciples and proclaims her news; she has seen the Lord, and He has spoken thus to her.

There are one or two remarkable features common to

the two narratives. In both there is a close similarity
between the words of Jesus and the words ascribed to the
angel or angels, although they are not the same words in
the two Gospels. If we emend the text of John,[1] Jesus in
both Gospels utters a word of reassurance, 'Fear not'.
If the text is allowed to stand, in both Gospels there is an
attempt expressed or implied to lay hold on Jesus. In
both there is a message to 'my brethren',[2] although its
content is entirely different in John. It is not difficult to
trace the genesis of the Johannine account. At the time
when the Gospel was written there was a tradition that
the woman who went to the sepulchre saw Jesus, and that
He sent by her a message to His brethren, or His disciples.
The author believed that the fact of the resurrection had
already been revealed to the two disciples, and he was
therefore embarrassed to give point to the conversation.
So he changed the original reference to the resurrection
into a reference to the ascension, which he apparently
regarded not as a distinct event, but as the completion of
the resurrection.[3] Yet he was still under the influence of
the earlier form of the tradition, for he makes the first
point of Mary's announcement the declaration that she
had seen the Lord, and therefore that He was risen from
the dead.

[1] μὴ πτόου for μὴ ἅπτου.
[2] A few MSS read μαθηταῖς for ἀδελφοῖς in Matthew. If that reading
is correct, then ἀδελφοῖς is due to assimilation to John.
[3] References to the ascension in the Fourth Gospel are mysterious
(cp. vi. 62). It is just possible that an account was omitted when
chapter xxi was added to the Gospel, but more probably the Gospel
represents a stage in the growth of tradition when the ascension had
not become wholly distinguished from the resurrection. In that respect
it is 'earlier' than Acts, and perhaps earlier than Luke.

This analysis of the Johannine account shows the state
of tradition at the time the author wrote. There had been
great development along several lines, and he tried to
make one consistent narrative out of different presenta-
tions of what had once been the same tradition. This may
be good evidence that the composition of the Fourth
Gospel must be put fairly late, although it must always
be borne in mind that we do not know how rapidly
tradition developed in certain circles; but it is no evidence
at all that the author had read the other Gospels, which
all present accounts inconsistent with his in one way or
another.

John xx. 19–29

The Fourth Gospel, like the Third, is committed to a belief
that Jesus appeared to His disciples in Jerusalem on the
day of the resurrection. Here, say the less cautious critics,
we have a clear indication that the author was acquainted
with St Luke's Gospel.

Let us note the particulars in which the two Gospels
agree, and in what respects they are at variance. They
agree that the disciples were assembled on the Sunday
evening at Jerusalem, an agreement which is important
inasmuch as it is most unlikely to represent an historical
fact. From other evidence we may judge that after the
crucifixion the disciples were scattered,[1] and it was not
until they had returned from Galilee that they assembled

---

[1] There can surely be no doubt which is to be preferred, the
Jerusalem or the Galilee tradition. The earliest evangelist, Mark, clearly
knew nothing of an immediate appearance in Jerusalem, and Matthew
was equally ignorant. It is easy to see how the Galilee tradition
became that which told of an appearance in Jerusalem; it is most
unlikely that the change would have been in the other direction.

in Jerusalem. But the Jerusalem tradition is easily explained. In some quarters it was considered incredible that the risen Lord should have allowed His disciples to wait until they had returned to Galilee for a revelation of His continued presence, and so the belief grew up that He had appeared in Jerusalem on the first day of the week. To that extent it is clear that the Third and Fourth Gospels belong to the same family, but Lk. xxiv. 34: 'The Lord is risen indeed and hath appeared unto Simon', betrays the fact that originally the Lucan story referred to a later occasion when the news of the Lord's appearance to Peter in Galilee had reached Jerusalem.

The two Gospels agree also in stating that Jesus convinced the disciples of His identity by showing to them His hands and His side or feet. They agree too in representing this as the occasion on which Jesus gave His commission to His Church.

But the differences between the two Gospels are far more remarkable. The Fourth Gospel represents the disciples as met together behind locked doors, a detail of which there is no hint in Luke, who seems to think of the two who walked to Emmaus as joining the other disciples without difficulty, and who is at particular pains to insist on the substantiality of the body of Jesus. The Fourth Evangelist says nothing of the fear of the disciples, which is emphasized by Luke. 'Therefore the disciples were glad' is more than a free paraphrase of Lk. xxiv. 41, 'and while they were unbelieving for joy'. 'As my Father hath sent me, even so send I you' has little in common with Lk. xxiv. 46, 'And he said unto them, Thus it is written that the Christ should suffer and rise again from

the dead on the third day, and that repentance unto
remission of sins should be preached in his name unto all
the nations.'

No doubt it might be thought that in these particulars the
Fourth Evangelist has introduced deliberate alterations,
but in verses 22 and 23 the contradiction of the Lucan
account is so fundamental that it becomes very difficult
to believe that the author was familiar with our Third
Gospel. 'And having thus spoken he breathed and saith
to them, Receive ye Holy Spirit; whosesover sins ye remit
they are remitted to them; whosoever sins ye retain they
are retained.' This is St John's conclusion to the ministry
of Jesus, and the meaning cannot be in doubt. Jesus, now
departing, bequeaths His Spirit to His disciples, the
Christian Church. In the power of that Spirit they will
continue His work, granting or withholding baptism, and
therefore remission of sins, as the Spirit dictates.[1] How
different is Luke's conception! He too believes that the
work of the Church began with the gift of the Holy Spirit,
but he thinks of that as a subsequent event for which
the disciples are expressly warned to wait at Jerusalem.
'Behold I send the promise of my Father upon you; do
ye wait in the city until ye be endued with power from
on high.' It is in the highest degree improbable that the
Fourth Evangelist would have written as he did if he had
read the Lucan account. He was clearly using a tradition
which had diverged from the common stream before
Luke wrote his Gospel.

Moreover, John's tradition has developed in a manner
unknown to Luke. In the following verses he relates an

[1] Cp. Mt. xxviii. 19, Lk. xxiv. 46, 47.

incident for which there is no room in the Third Gospel. The appearance on the following Sunday is something of an anticlimax, for the Church has already received its commission and the gift of the Spirit in whose power it is to carry out its work. Yet the story must have had considerable evidential value, and its omission by the other evangelists is conclusive proof that they did not know it.

John xxi. 1–14

We have already remarked that the Fourth Gospel contains some traces of traditions more primitive that those embodied in Matthew and Luke. Whatever may be the origin of chapter xxi and its relation to the rest of the Gospel, it is historically of the greatest interest. Without warning we are transported to Galilee, where we find Peter and six other disciples following their old calling as fishermen, apparently unaware of the resurrection. To them Jesus appears in the early morning. He enables them to make a great catch of fish, and joins them in a simple meal.

That this is no part of the original account of the Fourth Gospel is sufficiently apparent, in spite of the statement of verse 1 that '*After these things* Jesus showed himself again to the disciples at the sea of Tiberias', and in spite of verse 14, 'This is now the third time that Jesus was manifested to the disciples after that he was risen from the dead'. These are clearly editorial touches. We may trace three stages in the growth of the Johannine tradition. In the first, the appearance in the locked room was final; then was added the story of the subsequent appearance to Thomas; finally this account of an appearance by the sea of Tiberias was added as an appendix, but little attempt was made to bring it into agreement with what had already been written, still less to reconcile it with the account of Luke.

It has often been suggested that the source of Jn. xxi was the lost ending of Mark. If by that is meant that the Fourth Evangelist had actually seen an unmutilated copy of our Second Gospel the suggestion must be decisively rejected; the style is thoroughly Johannine, and the names of the seven disciples were never derived from a synoptic source. But it is none the less true that Jn. xxi takes us back to a form of the tradition of the resurrection such as seems to be anticipated in Mk. xvi. 7, and which is more primitive than the traditions embodied in the First and Third Gospels. The disciples are back in Galilee, still uninformed concerning the resurrection; they have resumed their work as fishermen; Jesus appears almost as though walking on the water; Peter is specially prominent in the subsequent scene, and he is given a commission, not indeed as a fisher of men, but as a pastor of the sheep of Christ. This is just the kind of conclusion to which we may judge that Mark was leading, and there is every reason to suppose that it represents a very early form of the tradition of the resurrection. It appears also in *The Gospel of Peter*.

Why was this chapter, a survival of the beliefs of an earlier generation, added to the Fourth Gospel by the original author or by 'one of his school'? No certain answer is possible, but we may guess that in the circle for which he wrote the old tradition was not altogether forgotten; it did not fit in well with the later traditions

which St John accepted as true, and at first he was
inclined to omit it; but the omission was noticed and
resented, and a compromise was reached by adding it as
an appendix. Let it be noted that no very late date is
here implied. In Luke's circle the tradition of an appearance by the lake in Galilee could be ignored, replaced as
it was by the later story of an appearance in Jerusalem.
In Matthew's time the Galilean appearance still survived
as a vague memory, but hardly anything was known
about it, and Peter's part in the scene had been forgotten.
If we could be sure that the development of tradition
proceeded at the same rate in all the churches we might
even conclude that the appendix to St John's Gospel was
written earlier than either Matthew or Luke.

However that may be, there is clearly no suggestion
here of dependence upon either of the other Gospels, and
those who believe that Luke has left his mark upon the
later chapters of the Fourth Gospel may well be called
upon to explain how it is that an appendix is added to
St John which is plainly contradictory of the Third Gospel.

Another point arises. Combined with the story of the
appearance of Jesus is the story of the miraculous draught
of fishes which Luke also has but which he combines with
his account of the call of Peter in chapter v. Is it likely
that the author of Jn. xxi would have combined this story
with that of the restoration of Simon Peter[1] if he had known
that in a document so important as the Third Gospel it
had already been combined with the narrative of Peter's
call? It is indeed strange that some critics should appeal
to the fact that this story appears in both Gospels in

[1] In the passage in Lk. v also Peter is called 'Simon Peter'.

support of the theory that John is dependent upon Luke. Both evangelists evidently knew the story of the miraculous draught, but they are quite independent in the use that they make of it. The fact that they used it in such different contexts comes near to proving that neither was acquainted with the work of the other.

Of the two, John is if anything the more primitive, for in his version the allegorical origin of the story is still discernible; the fish number one hundred and fifty and three, and the net does not break; all nations are to be brought into the net of the Church, and there will be room for all. In Luke the story is presented simply as a miracle and nothing more.

Yet another primitive element is to be found in the account of the meal, where the elements of the Eucharist are bread and fish. This takes us back behind the synoptic association of the origin of the Eucharist with the Last Supper, behind I Corinthians, to a very early time when Christians shared their meal, whatever it might be, in continuation of the custom of the Lord during the months of the ministry.

John xxi. 15–23

The concluding verses of the chapter introduce many problems with which we are not here concerned, but they throw no light upon the relationship of the Fourth Gospel to the other three. They take us back to a time after the death of Peter when his memory as the shepherd of the flock of Christ was still fresh in the memory of the Church.

Chapter VII

CONCLUSION

IT REMAINS to gather up the threads of our argument, and to draw any conclusions that seem possible.

A close examination of those passages in the Fourth Gospel which have any parallels in the other three reveals some agreement and a great deal of disagreement between them. The attention of critics has generally been concentrated on the points of agreement, and insufficient regard has been paid to the very important divergences which are everywhere apparent. When all the facts are taken into consideration it becomes difficult to believe that the author of the Fourth Gospel was familiar with those Gospels which are generally thought to have been written and given to the Church before he undertook his task. Perhaps some of those who have followed our examination may be surprised to find how slender is the evidence on which the common belief of St John's dependence upon the Synoptists rests, and how weighty are the objections to be urged against it, even in the case of Mark.

The theory that John knew our Second Gospel is generally based on two considerations. In the first place, it is said that his general scheme and order are the same as Mark's, whereas if his work had been independent we should have expected an entirely different presentation of the life of Christ. This argument not only exaggerates the similarity of the Fourth Gospel to the Synoptic Gospels, but also ignores the conditions of its composition so far as they can be determined. Of late years it has come to be realized that early Christian tradition was from the first arranged in some kind of order in accordance with the needs and conventions of the Apostolic Preaching. Christian evangelism was not carried out in any haphazard manner, but the Good News of Christ was presented in accordance with a definite plan. The facts of the life and death of Jesus were related, not as interesting stories, still less as the result of scientific research, but as illustrations of the great truths of the Gospel. That being so, they inevitably fell into some kind of order. The career of John the Baptist the forerunner of the Christ, was described to illustrate the great theme of the fulfilment of prophecy. The ministry of Jesus in Galilee and Judaea was related because it revealed Him as the Messiah, acclaimed by demons, manifested in works of power, confessed by disciples, denied by Jews. The climax was always the narrative of the crucifixion and resurrection, for thereby the claims of Jesus were vindicated, the wickedness of the Jews revealed, and the certainty of judgment and salvation to come established. Thus the outline of any written Gospel was determined not only by the natural sequence of history, but also by the form of the Preaching of the Apostles and their immediate followers.

It is possible to go further. By the time when the Gospels came to be written there must have been considerable development within this outline, and in the local churches many sections of the tradition had probably fallen into an accepted order.[1] No doubt there was much

[1] For instance, it may have been customary at quite an early period to relate the story of Christ's walking on the water immediately after the story of the feeding of the five thousand.

variety in the different churches, but as time passed the general tendency would be towards uniformity in the sequence of the sections. Possibly written works, now lost, were not without influence; for if, as St Luke says, many had taken in hand the task of providing a connected account, their work must have contributed to the establishment of a standard form of written Gospel.

It is not surprising therefore that St John produced an account which agrees in some of its main features with the Synoptic Gospels, and the fact provides little ground for concluding that he was acquainted with the work of Mark. When the conditions of the latter part of the first century are considered it will be realized that a wholly 'independent' account was hardly possible outside the irresponsible circles which produced the Apocryphal Gospels.

The argument to which more attention is generally paid is that which depends upon a recognition of small and apparently unimportant points of agreement between St John and the Synoptists, the common use of words and phrases, references to persons and matters which the author has not himself mentioned, and in general the assumption underlying his narrative that his readers were not without knowledge of the history of the ministry. We have reviewed this argument in most of its particular applications, and in view of all that has been said the reader must estimate its weight. Our contention is that the theory of literary dependence, which has proved fruitful in the field of synoptic criticism, has been misapplied in the study of St John. Critics have often overlooked an important distinction. Certain facts may prove that the Fourth Evangelist was familiar with some of the traditions used by the Synoptists, but it does not necessarily follow that he had read the Synoptic Gospels. Whoever he was and whenever he wrote the evangelist certainly lived in a Christian environment, and he was familiar with Christian practices, Christian beliefs, and a Christian vocabulary. Probably he adapted accepted traditions to suit his own purpose, but he did not invent the stories which he tells, and if in relating incidents also recorded in one or more of the other Gospels he sometimes used a word or a phrase which appears also in them, it proves no more than that all the evangelists drew upon the common store of Christian tradition. It may be surprising that the common store was so limited, but that it existed can hardly be denied.

It is in dealing with the evidence of words and phrases that critical method has often been at fault. Nearly all discussions of the relationship of St John to the Synoptists proceed upon the same lines. Points of similarity are picked out and discussed in isolation; it is concluded that John must have known Mark, or Mark and Luke; then, when the matter has been thus decided, an attempt is made to account for some of the much more numerous discrepancies between several Gospels. Thus, the late Dr Streeter, having reached his conclusion by the 'microscopic examination' of selected passages, goes on to admit that 'a standing difficulty of New Testament scholarship has always been to explain why the author of the Fourth Gospel goes out of his way, as it were, to differ from the Synoptists on points of no theological significance'.[1] May

[1] Streeter, *op. cit.* p. 417.

it not be that the standing difficulty has been set upon its feet by scholars themselves? His admission should have warned Dr Streeter that something might be wrong with his original conclusion, and with the method by which it had been reached. It is not a scientific proceeding to form a conclusion on one half of the evidence, and then to force the other half into agreement with it. The passages in which there are correspondences between St John and the Synoptists do not stand alone and should not be considered by themselves; indeed they form a small minority among the far more numerous passages in which the discrepancies are many and glaring. The problem must be decided on all the evidence considered together, and when that is done there can be little doubt on which side the balance of probability inclines. Agreement between two documents can nearly always be explained as due to the use of a common source, whether oral or written; but if literary dependence is assumed it is extremely difficult to explain pointless contradictions. The present author finds it inconceivable that St John was content wantonly to contradict the testimony of 'standard works' in matters dogmatically indifferent. Sometimes he may have known himself to have been better informed than other teachers, sometimes he may have rejected a tradition because he did not like it, just as Matthew and Luke did, but there are many passages in which he differs from the Synoptists for no apparent reason, and of them the easiest explanation is certainly ignorance.

The question of the indebtedness of St John to the Synoptists is of much more than academic interest, for it leads on to further questions concerning the date and authority of the Fourth Gospel. It is not the purpose of this short work to discuss these questions at length, but a few words may be added in conclusion.

Firstly, with regard to the date of St John, if once it is admitted that the Evangelist shows no positive signs of acquaintance with the synoptic writers it can no longer be assumed that his is literally the *Fourth* Gospel. It is just conceivable that its later and more developed tone is due to the fact that it was produced in some locality in which development had been more rapid than in other parts of the Church. Professor Stanton's words are worth quoting: 'The interval between the composition of the Fourth Gospel and the two later Synoptics need not have been more than one or two decades, if so much, and they were probably produced in other parts of the Christian Church.' It has too often been assumed that what development took place in tradition and theology was uniform throughout the world, whereas the opposite is likely to have been the case.

The form-critics have drawn attention to the conditions of the period in which the Gospel traditions took shape. During that period all that was known about the life of Jesus was embodied in oral traditions, and inevitably there must have been growth in accordance with local conditions and to meet the needs of local communities. Tradition would not develop always in the same direction or at the same rate. From the first some churches would be better informed than others, and as time passed they would have better opportunities of increasing their knowledge. Christianity spread rapidly in the great centres of population, and although the majority of the early believers were men of humble station, yet it cannot have been long before the Gospel reached circles in which higher education prevailed. St Paul preached to philosophers at Athens, and in cities like Alexandria and Ephesus a few converts would soon be made among men of culture. Their influence would certainly be important, and they would raise the general intellectual level of the local church.

We realize now that all the Gospels represent an interpretation and not only a presentation of the facts, and the interpretation produced, for instance, at Alexandria, could not be the same as that which gained currency at Antioch or Rome. Among believers well versed in the philosophical ideas of the age there would inevitably be an attempt to relate the essentials of the Gospel preaching to current philosophy, and the 'simple gospel' would be rapidly absorbed in some inclusive gnosis. The development of theology would react upon the development of tradition, and before long the stories about Jesus told in some great centre of culture would differ considerably from the stories related in a Syrian village.

This difference of *tempo* in the various churches has an important bearing upon the problem of the date of St John's Gospel. In a sense it is undoubtedly the latest of the four, embodying a far more advanced theology than that of Matthew or Luke; but if St John was indeed independent it is not quite certain that his lateness of tone implies a corresponding lateness in time. To take a parallel case, it would be most unsafe to argue that because the earliest Christianity was Jewish, and St Matthew's Gospel is Jewish in tone, therefore it was written earlier than St Luke's, which is clearly addressed to Christians in the Gentile world. Have we any more right to conclude, as did Clement of Alexandria, from the spiritual and philosophical tone of the Fourth Gospel that it must have been written later than the Synoptics in which the element of interpretation is less conspicuous? St John gives us an account of the life of Christ such as would appeal to the πνευματικοί of his age, an amalgam of history and philosophy, with the latter predominating; but it may not have required a very long period for such an interpretation to be developed in one or two centres of Hellenistic learning.

On the other hand, the primitive elements which crop up from time to time in the Gospel must be given full weight. In the last few years there has been a distinct tendency to admit that in some respects the Fourth Gospel is nearer to primitive tradition than either Matthew or Luke.[1] We do not know the date of St Mark with any certainty, and as to the date of the other Synoptists there is very little evidence, but few critics would put them much earlier than A.D. 85–90. Is there any compelling reason for supposing that St John is much later? Is it certain that he must be put so late? If Matthew and Luke knew Mark, and John did not, there is a *prima facie* case for putting the Fourth Gospel before the First and Third. Indeed, we might tentatively suggest that Mark and John were almost contemporaries. Vastly more thinking

---

[1] 'In the Fourth Gospel we can discern, no less clearly than in Mark, and even more clearly than in Matthew or Luke, the fixed outline of the *kerugma* as we have it in Acts x and xiii.' Professor Dodd goes on to show how much there is in common between the Marcan and the Johannine schemes. *The Apostolic Preaching*, p. 164.

lies behind the Fourth Gospel than behind the Second,
but that does not necessarily imply that it was written
at a much later date. There is more thinking behind the
Epistle to the Romans than behind the Epistle of St
James, but the probability remains that Romans is very
much the earlier document. The character of a book
depends upon its author more than upon its date, and the
author of the Fourth Gospel was quite a different man
from St Mark, living in a different intellectual atmosphere
and writing for a different public. It is true that the
traditions on which he worked were 'later' traditions
than those incorporated in the Second Gospel, but that
may mean no more than that they had developed more
rapidly, like plants in a hothouse, which soon outgrow
those in an open garden.

This is admittedly speculative, and it is not claimed
that the evidence for an early date for this Gospel is
compelling. But the problem, no longer encumbered by
the false assumption of St John's dependence upon the
Synoptists, is worthy of fresh investigation.

Secondly, there emerges a new possibility of regarding
the Fourth Gospel as an independent authority for
the life of Jesus, or at least for the traditions current
in the Christian Church in the second half of the first
century. So long as it was believed that John knew Mark,
and altered his account in an arbitrary and irresponsible
manner, interest in him as a historian could never be great.
But if in the Fourth Gospel we have a survival of a type
of first century Christianity which owed nothing to synoptic
developments, and which originated in quite a different
intellectual atmosphere, its historical value may be very

great indeed. Not that critics are likely to accept the Johannine account as historical in the narrower sense of the term; the influence of interpretation is too obvious for that; but where the Fourth Gospel differs from the Synoptics it may henceforth be wise to treat its testimony with rather more respect than it has lately received, and perhaps in not a few cases it may prove to be right.

It is not to be expected that the arguments here presented will win universal assent, or even wide approval; but perhaps enough has been said to justify the claim that the relation of St John to the synoptic writers is worthy of a fresh examination. If the view should gain ground that the Fourth Gospel, whatever its authorship and date, is an independent work, then a new chapter will have opened in the criticism of the Gospels and the study of Christian origins.

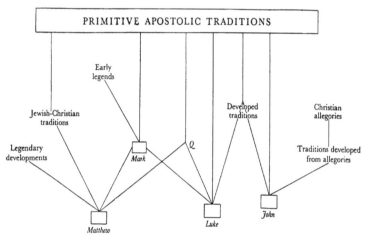

PRIMITIVE APOSTOLIC TRADITIONS

Early
legends

Jewish-Christian
traditions

Developed
traditions

Christian
allegories

Legendary
developments

Mark

Q

Traditions developed
from allegories

Matthew

Luke

John

Derivation does not exclude development in the case of oral tradition.

Certain documents may have been used in the composition of the Gospels—an apocalyptic document by Mark, and written Passion narratives by Mark, Luke and John.

THE SOURCES OF THE GOSPELS

INDEX

Made in the USA
Columbia, SC
01 April 2021

35422331R00071